Teaching Study Skills and Strategies in College

Related Titles of Interest

Getting the Most Out of College
Arthur W. Chickering and Nancy K. Schlossberg
ISBN: 0-205-14890-5

How to Succeed in College
Robert DiYanni
ISBN: 0-205-17526-0

Learning to Learn: Making the Transition from Student to Learner
Ken Kiewra and Nelson F. DuBois
ISBN: 0-205-26319-4

College Study Strategies: Thinking and Learning
Marcia L. Laskey and Paula W. Gibson
ISBN: 0-205-19152-5

Cornerstone: Building on Your Best
Rhonda J. Montgomery, Patricia G. Moody and Robert M. Sherfield
ISBN: 0-205-18578-9

Also of Interest

Teaching Study Skills and Strategies in High School
Stephen S. Strichart, Charles T. Mangrum II, and Patricia Iannuzzi
ISBN: 0-205-19881-3

Teaching Study Skills and Strategies in Grades 4–8
Charles T. Mangrum II, Patricia Iannuzzi, and Stephen S. Strichart
ISBN 0-205-19879-1

Teaching Study Skills and Strategies to Students Who Are LD, ADD, or At-Risk, Second Edition
Stephen S. Strichart, Charles T. Mangrum II, and Patricia Iannuzzi
ISBN: 0-205-27469-2

For more information or to purchase a book, please call 1-800-278-3525.

Teaching Study Skills and Strategies in College

PATRICIA IANNUZZI
Florida International University

STEPHEN S. STRICHART
Florida International University

CHARLES T. MANGRUM II
University of Miami–Coral Gables

Allyn and Bacon
Boston London Toronto Sydney Tokyo Singapore

Credits

Publisher: Nancy Forsyth
Series editorial assistant: Cheryl Ouellette
Advertising manager: Anne Morrison
Manufacturing buyer: Suzanne Lareau

Internet: www.abacon.com
America Online: keyword: College Online

Some of the activities in this book have been adapted from *Teaching Study Strategies to Students with Learning Disabilities,* by Stephen S. Strichart and Charles T. Mangrum II, copyright © 1993 by Allyn & Bacon.

Library of Congress Cataloging-in-Publication Data

Iannuzzi, Patricia.
Teaching study skills and strategies in college / Patricia Iannuzzi, Stephen S. Strichart, Charles T. Mangrum II.
p. cm.
Includes bibliographical references (p.).
ISBN 0-205-26817-X
1. Study skills—Handbooks, manuals, etc. 2. Test-taking skills—Handbooks, manuals, etc. 3. Note-taking—Handbooks, manuals, etc. 4. College students—Time management—Handbooks, manuals, etc. 5. Report writing—Handbooks, manuals, etc. I. Strichart, Stephen S. II. Mangrum, Charles T. III. Title.
LB2395.I25 1998
378.1'7'028'1—dc21 97-30229
CIP

Printed in the United States of America

10 9 8 7 6 5 4 3 2 1 01 00 99 98 97

Contents

Introduction

This book contains reproducible activities for teaching the study skills and strategies important for success in college. The reproducible activities can be used for class instruction or can be assigned to students for independent learning. Included with this book is a trial version of a computer assessment that can be used to identify instructional needs of students.

HOW THIS BOOK IS ORGANIZED

This book contains seven chapters:

Chapter One
Remembering Information

In this chapter, we show how to use eight techniques to remember important information. Repetition is presented for remembering information that is not very detailed, mnemonic techniques (acronyms, abbreviations, acronymic sentences, pegwords, keywords, rhyme) for information that is detailed, and graphic organizers for information that is very detailed.

Chapter Two
Reading and Taking Notes from Textbooks Using SQ4R

In this chapter, we show how to use a textbook reading and notetaking strategy called SQ4R. Students are taken through the six steps in SQ4R: Survey, Question, Read, wRite, Recite, Review.

Chapter Three
Taking Notes in Class

In this chapter, we present a strategy for taking class notes. The strategy guides students through the three notetaking stages of what they. should do before they take notes, while they take notes, and after they take notes. Students are also taught to identify and take notes for the different lecture styles used by college instructors: Topic–List, Question–Answer, Compare–Contrast, Series of Events, Cause–Effect, Problem–Solution.

Chapter Four
Using Information Literacy Skills to Do Research

In this chapter, we show how to use the library and the Internet to identify, locate, and evaluate information in all formats. Students also learn to use print and electronic tools. They then learn how to locate a wide variety of sources and formats of information for their own research projects. Finally, we present methods for evaluating the information they find.

Chapter Five
Writing a Research Paper

In this chapter, we present a ten-step strategy for students to follow, step by step, in writing a research paper. We show how to choose appropriate topics, locate information, and document sources in footnotes and a bibliography.

Chapter Six
Preparing for and Taking Tests

In this chapter, we present a five-day strategy for preparing for tests. We show strategies for doing well on the following types of tests: essay, multiple-choice, true/false, matching, completion.

Chapter Seven
Managing Time and Space

In this chapter, we show how to evaluate one's study habits and study place. We present ideas for improving study habits and study place and for managing time using a Semester Calendar and a daily To Do List.

Each chapter is organized as follows:

1. Objectives
2. Titles of Reproducible Activities
3. Using Reproducible Activities
4. Reproducible Activities
5. Answer Key

COMPUTER ASSESSMENT

Accompanying this book is a trial version of a computer assessment titled **Study Skills and Strategies Assessment—College Level (3S-C)**. 3S-C assesses students' use of the study skills and strategies taught in this book. The free trial disk, available in Windows only, allows you to administer 3S-C to five students. 3S-C generates a Diagnostic Profile and a Narrative Report for each student assessed. The trial disk is no longer usable after five administrations. You may then purchase a disk with either 50 or unlimited administrations, available in both Windows and Macintosh versions. The Order Form is found on page 157.

HOW TO USE THIS BOOK

1. Assess the study skills and strategies of your students. You can use 3S-C to do this. Use the results of the assessments to select the chapters most appropriate for your students.
2. Duplicate the reproducible activities you wish to use.
3. Follow the suggestions in "Using Reproducible Activities" at the beginning of each chapter.
4. Have your students complete activities in or out of class.
5. Use the Answer Key to check your students' answers.
6. Readminister the assessments to evaluate students' progress.

Acknowledgments

We express our appreciation to our colleagues at the University of Miami and Florida International University who graciously gave their time to review the activities in this book. Their reactions and recommendations were of great assistance to us. We also wish to acknowledge our university students. Their feedback about the activities allowed us to make important improvements.

About the Authors

This work is the equal and shared product of the following authors:

Patricia Iannuzzi is University Librarian and Head of the Reference Department at Florida International University Libraries. She graduated from Yale University and earned an M.S. in Library and Information Science at Simmons College in 1980. Ms. Iannuzzi has worked in libraries at Tufts University, Yale University, and the University of California at Berkeley. Since 1990, she has been on the library faculty at Florida International University, where she teaches study skills and strategies to freshmen. She also teaches information literacy skills in subjects across the curriculum.

Stephen S. Strichart is professor of special education and learning disabilities at Florida International University, Miami. He graduated from City College of New York and taught children with various types of disabilities before entering graduate school. Dr. Strichart earned a Ph.D. from Yeshiva University in 1972. Since 1975, he has been on the faculty at Florida International University, where he trains teachers and psychologists to work with exceptional students. Dr. Strichart is the author of many books and articles on topics related to special education and study skills.

Charles T. Mangrum II is professor of special education and reading at the University of Miami, Coral Gables, Florida. He graduated from Northern Michigan University and taught elementary and secondary school before entering graduate school. He earned an Ed.D. from Indiana University in 1968. Since 1968, he has been on the faculty at the University of Miami, where he trains teachers who teach students with reading and learning disabilities. Dr. Mangrum is the author of many books, instructional programs, and articles on topics related to reading and study skills.

Teaching Study Skills and Strategies in College

CHAPTER ONE

Remembering Information

OBJECTIVES

1. **Teach students to use repetition to remember information that is not very detailed.**
2. **Teach students to use mnemonic techniques to remember information that is detailed.**
3. **Teach students to use graphic organizers to remember information that is very detailed.**

REPRODUCIBLE ACTIVITIES

1-1 Techniques for Remembering Information
1-2 Using Repetition to Remember Information
1-3 Learning about Mnemonics: Acronyms
1-4 Using Acronyms
1-5 Learning about Mnemonics: Abbreviations
1-6 Using Abbreviations
1-7 Learning about Mnemonics: Acronymic Sentences
1-8 Using Acronymic Sentences
1-9 Learning about Mnemonics: Pegwords
1-10 Using Pegwords
1-11 Learning about Mnemonics: Keywords
1-12 Using Keywords
1-13 Learning about Mnemonics: Rhyme
1-14 Using Rhyme
1-15 Learning about Graphic Organizers: Topic List
1-16 Learning about Graphic Organizers: Question–Answer
1-17 Learning about Graphic Organizers: Compare–Contrast
1-18 Learning about Graphic Organizers: Series of Events
1-19 Learning about Graphic Organizers: Cause–Effect
1-20 Learning about Graphic Organizers: Problem–Solution
Answer Key

USING REPRODUCIBLE ACTIVITIES

Here is a plan for using the chapter reproducible activities. Activities may be completed by students either independently or in class.

1. Use 1-1 to introduce students to eight techniques for remembering information.
2. Use 1-2 to teach students how to use repetition for remembering information that is not very detailed.
3. Use 1-3 through 1-14 to teach students how to use six mnemonic techniques for remembering information that is detailed.
4. Use 1-15 through 1-20 to teach students how to construct graphic organizers for remembering information that is very detailed.

Techniques for Remembering Information **1-1**

Here are eight techniques for remembering information. The technique you should use depends on the number of details you must remember. Read to learn about these techniques and when to use them. Then answer the questions.

Repetition When you read, say, or write information a number of times, you are using repetition. Repetition is most useful for remembering information that is **not very detailed**.

Mnemonics To remember information that is **detailed**, you should use a mnemonic. Here are several mnemonics from which you can choose.

- **Acronyms** are words formed by using the first letters of information to be remembered. The acronym does not have to be a real word, but it must be pronounceable.
- **Abbreviations** are formed by using the first letters of each word of the information to be remembered. An abbreviation does not form a pronounceable word.
- **Acronymic sentences** are sentences formed from words that begin with the first letter of each word of the information to be remembered.
- **Pegwords** are words that rhyme with numbers and are used to build associations with information to be remembered.
- **Keywords** are familiar words that sound like words to be learned. They can be used to create mental images that you can use to remember new words and their definitions.
- **Rhymes** are poems or verses used to remember information.

Graphic Organizers When information to be remembered is **very detailed**, you may need to use a graphic organizer. Graphic organizers are visual representations that show how information is organized.

Which technique(s) should you use to remember the following:

1. Information that is detailed?

2. Information that is not very detailed?

3. Information that is very detailed?

Using Repetition to Remember Information

1-2

Repetition is most useful when the information to be remembered is *not very detailed*. When you read, say, or write information a number of times to remember it, you are using repetition. Here are the steps to follow when using repetition:

Repetition Procedure

1. Read the information aloud.
2. Close your eyes and repeat the information.
3. Write the information from memory.
4. Repeat the steps at least three times or until you can remember the information without error.

Read each of the following statements about information to be remembered. Write "repetition" after each statement that is not very detailed and for which you would use repetition to remember the information.

1. You have to remember the date a certain event happened.

2. You have to remember the names of ten provinces and two territories found in Canada.

3. You have to remember the name of the inventor of the computer chip.

4. You have to remember the organizational structure of the United States government.

5. You have to remember two characteristics of mammals.

6. You have to remember the definition of a word you know how to pronounce.

7. You have to remember seven chemicals used to produce a specific reaction.

Learning about Mnemonics: Acronyms 1-3

Mnemonics are used to remember information that is **detailed**.

Acronyms are words formed by using the first letters of information to be remembered. The acronym does not have to be a real word, but it must be pronounceable. For example, you might form the acronym HOMES to remember the names of the five Great Lakes: *H*uron, *O*ntario, *M*ichigan, *E*rie, *S*uperior.

Read the following information about global social stratification.

> The world consists of a number of nations, which can be stratified according to their power, prestige, and money. Most commonly, these nations are divided into three divisions according to how they rank in terms of wealth and industrialization. The countries of the First World, led by Switzerland, Austria, the United States, Luxembourg, and Canada, are the wealthiest and most industrialized. Countries in the Second World group, which includes Portugal, Greece, Indonesia, Mexico, and Yugoslavia, have less wealth and are less industrialized. The Third World group is the poorest group of nations and includes Bulgaria, Turkey, Argentina, Brazil, India, and Macedonia.

1. Write the first letter of the name of each First World country.

2. Arrange the letters to form an acronym.

3. Arrange the first letters of the Second World countries to form an acronym.

4. Form an acronym for remembering the Third World countries.

Using Acronyms **1-4**

1. Locate information in one of your textbooks or your class notes for which you would use an acronym to remember the information. Write the information here.

   See how many acronyms you can form using the first letter of each important fact or idea you need to remember.

   Which acronym do you prefer? Why?

2. Locate another set of information for which you would use an acronym to remember the information. Write the information here.

   Write your acronym.

Learning about Mnemonics: Abbreviations

1-5

Abbreviations are formed by using the first letters of important things to be remembered. Unlike an acronym, an abbreviation does not form a pronounceable word. Use the abbreviation technique when you cannot form an acronym.

The abbreviation NFCRBC can help you remember the names of the presidents of the United States in order from Nixon through Clinton. This abbreviation was formed using the first letter of the last name of each president. Use the abbreviation to recall and write their names in order.

1. N

   F

   C

   R

   B

   C

If you do not need to remember information in order, you can arrange the letters in the order easiest for you to remember.

2. Write the abbreviation you would use to remember the following four criteria used to determine social class: *wealth, power, prestige, status.*
3. Write the abbreviation you would use to remember, in order, the six most populated cities in the world.

New York	5th
Mexico City	2nd
Saõ Paulo	3rd
Osaka–Kobe–Kyoto	6th
Tokyo–Yokohama	1st
Seoul	4th

Using Abbreviations **1-6**

1. Locate information in one of your textbooks or your class notes for which you would use an abbreviation to remember the information. Write the information here.

   Write your abbreviation.

   Explain why you arranged the letters the way you did.

2. Locate more information for which you would use an abbreviation to remember the information. Write the information here.

   Write your abbreviation.

   Explain why you arranged the letters the way you did.

Learning about Mnemonics: Acronymic Sentences

1-7

Acronymic sentences are sentences formed from words that begin with the first letter of things to be remembered. For example, the acronymic sentence "*A*lice *a*nd *A*lan *p*layed *i*nside" can be used to remember the names of the five oceans: *A*tlantic, *P*acific, *I*ndian, *A*rctic, *A*ntarctic.

Write an acronymic sentence for each of the following. Be as creative as you like. In some cases you will have to create an acronymic sentence that will help you remember the information in a specific order. When you do not have to remember information in a specific order, you can change the order of the information to create an acronymic sentence.

1. Remember the five parts of the digestive system:

liver, stomach, colon, intestine, pancreas

2. Remember these six major rivers of the world:

Snake, Mississippi, Amazon, Congo, Nile, Hudson

3. Remember the names of the planets in our solar system in order, moving away from the sun:

Mercury, Venus, Earth, Mars, Jupiter, Saturn, Uranus, Neptune, Pluto

4. Remember the geologic time periods in order from the oldest to the most recent:

Precambrian, Paleozoic, Mesozoic, Cenozoic

5. Remember four hydrocarbons of the alkaline class:

methane, ethane, propane, butane

Using Acronymic Sentences **1-8**

1. Locate information in one of your textbooks or your class notes for which you would use an acronymic sentence to remember the information. Write the information here.

   Write your acronymic sentence.

2. Locate more information for which you would use an acronymic sentence to remember the information. Write the information here.

   Write your acronymic sentence.

Learning about Mnemonics: Pegwords

Pegwords are words that rhyme with numbers and are used to build associations with information to be remembered. Each pegword helps you recall an association, which in turn helps you recall important information you want to remember. The more pegwords you have memorized, the more associations you can make. The more associations you make, the more information you remember. Here are pegwords for the number words *one* through *ten*. You can substitute your own pegwords as long as each rhymes with a number word. If you need to remember more than ten things, create additional pegwords to help you do so.

Number Word	*Pegword*	*Number Word*	*Pegword*
one	run	six	sticks
two	shoe	seven	heaven
three	bee	eight	gate
four	door	nine	vine
five	hive	ten	hen

Here is an example of how pegwords are used to remember the ten rights granted under the Bill of Rights. The first is "freedom of religion." Form a picture in your mind that associates *run* (the pegword for one) with freedom of religion. You might picture a group of people *running* out of a church being chased by soldiers with guns.

This picture will remind you that the first right under the Bill of Rights is "freedom of religion." To remember this, think of the word *run*. The word *run* will bring back into mind your picture of people running from a church being chased by soldiers.

The second right is that "states can have a national guard." You can remember this by using the pegword *shoe* to form a picture of an armed soldier guarding a giant shoe.

Use the remaining pegwords to remember the other rights. Draw or describe the picture you will use to remember the information associated with each pegword.

Pegwords	*Rights*
three/bee	We don't have to give food or shelter to soldiers during peacetime.
four/door	Our homes can't be searched without a search warrant.
five/hive	A person can not be brought to trial without evidence.
six/sticks	A person accused of a crime has the right to a speedy trial.
seven/heaven	You have a right to a trial by a jury of your peers.
eight/gate	Punishment for a crime must not be excessive.
nine/vine	Workers have the right to strike.
ten/hen	States run the public schools.

Using Pegwords 1-10

Locate information in one of your textbooks or your class notes that you can remember by using pegwords. Write the information here.

Use as many pegwords as necessary to remember the information. Next to each pegword, draw or describe in words the mental image you will use to remember the information associated with the pegword.

one/run

two/shoe

three/bee

four/door

five/hive

six/sticks

seven/heaven

eight/gate

nine/vine

ten/hen

Learning about Mnemonics: Keywords **1-11**

Keywords are used to remember the meaning of new vocabulary words. A keyword is a familiar word that sounds like all or part of a new word. Here is how to use a keyword to learn the meaning of a new word.

1. Think of a keyword that sounds like part or all of a new word. The keyword must be one you can easily picture in your mind.

   For example, you might use the keyword lips to help you remember the meaning of the new vocabulary word ellipse (a flattened circle).

2. Use the keyword to form a picture in your mind that shows the meaning of the new word.

   For example, you might form a picture of a person whose lips are shaped like a flattened circle and about to kiss you.

3. When you encounter the new word, recall the keyword and the picture you formed in your mind to remember the meaning of the new word.

   For example, the picture of the person about to kiss you will help you remember that an ellipse is a flattened circle.

Use keywords to remember the meaning of the following new words.

1. **cholesterol:** A fat-like chemical substance manufactured in the body and consumed from foods of animal origins only.

   Write your keyword:

   Draw or describe your picture:

2. **ethnocentrism:** The use of one's own culture as a yardstick for judging the ways of other individuals or societies, usually resulting in a negative evaluation of their norms, behaviors, and values.

   Write your keyword:

   Draw or describe your picture:

Using Keywords

Locate four new vocabulary words whose meaning you want to remember. Write each word to be learned, its definition, and your keyword. Then draw your picture or describe it in writing.

1. Word to be learned:

   Definition:

   Keyword:

   Picture:

2. Word to be learned:

   Definition:

   Keyword:

   Picture:

3. Word to be learned:

   Definition:

   Keyword:

   Picture:

4. Word to be learned:

   Definition:

   Keyword:

   Picture:

Learning about Mnemonics: Rhyme **1-13**

You can use rhymes to remember information. Here are two rhymes you may have learned to use a long time ago to remember information.

In fourteen hundred ninety-two
Columbus sailed the ocean blue.

Thirty days hath September
April, June, and November.

You do not have to be a poet to make rhymes. Let your imagination run wild. If you can create a rhyme that works for you, use it. If you can not create a rhyme, use one of the other remembering techniques.

Here is a rhyme for remembering who wrote *King Lear.*

Do you know a play by Shakespeare?
Absolutely, he wrote King Lear.

Create a rhyme for each of the following. Whenever you can't, write NO CAN RHYME!

1. Lansing is the capital of Michigan.

2. Jefferson was president of the United States when the Louisiana Purchase was made.

3. The Ice Age ended 10,000 years ago.

4. Objects that have like electric charges repel each other.

5. A literacy test is a test to determine if a person can read and write.

6. A black hole is matter so dense that not even light can escape its gravity.

7. A feeling of tightness in the throat is a common symptom of "acute grief syndrome."

8. According to Freud, the *id* consists of all our primitive, innate drives.

Using Rhyme

1-14

1. Locate information in one of your textbooks or your class notes that you can remember by forming a rhyme. Write the information here.

   Write your rhyme here.

2. Write some more information to be remembered.

   Write your rhyme here.

Learning about Graphic Organizers: Topic–List

1-15

Graphic organizers are useful for remembering information that is **very detailed**. They show graphically how information is organized. Here are six types of graphic organizers: topic–list, question–answer, compare–contrast, series of events, cause–effect, and problem–solution.

A **topic–list** graphic organizer shows how a topic, subtopics, and details are organized. Here are the questions you should answer to obtain the information needed to create a topic–list graphic organizer:

1. What is the topic?
2. What subtopics are related to the topic?
3. What details are known about the subtopics?

Read the following class notes about the determinants of social status. Then examine the topic–list graphic organizer for the notes.

> Determinants of social status. According to Karl Marx—two status levels: those who have (owners) means of production have high status. Others (workers) low status. According to Max Weber, social status determined by how much property (land and buildings) you own, your job, and level of education.

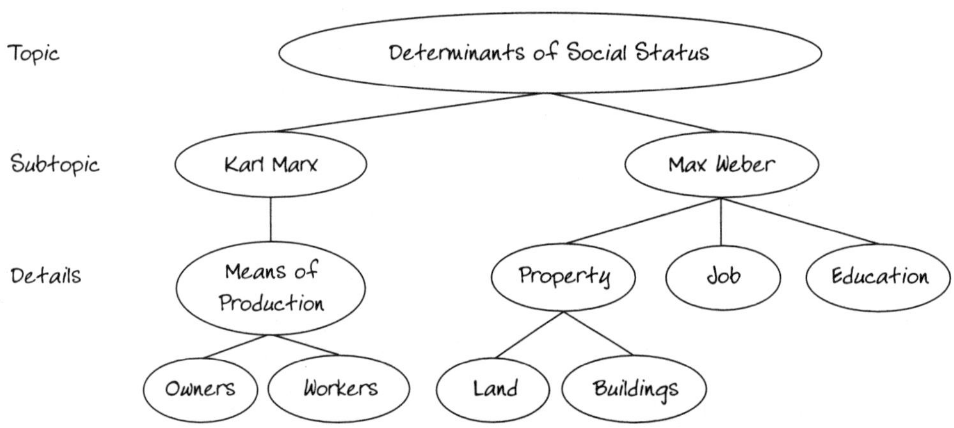

Create a topic–list graphic organizer for information you want to remember.

Learning about Graphic Organizers: Question–Answer

1-16

A **question–answer** graphic organizer shows how one or more questions, the answer for each, and supporting details for the answers are organized. Here are the questions you should answer to obtain the information needed to create a question–answer graphic organizer:

1. What is the topic?
2. What is/are the question(s)?
3. What is/are the answer(s)?
4. What details are known about the answer(s)?

Read the following class notes about agriculture in Norway. Then examine the question–answer graphic organizer for the notes.

> Why is Norway not a major agricultural country? An examination of a map of the world reveals that Norway is located in the far north. Because of its geographical location, the growing season is very short. Glaciers from the Ice Age left the soil thin and stony. This makes it very difficult to grow crops. The moist climate further limits the types of crops that can be grown. Major crops include potatoes and grains. Large agricultural machines cannot be used to work much of the land. Most of the farming must be done using hand tools.

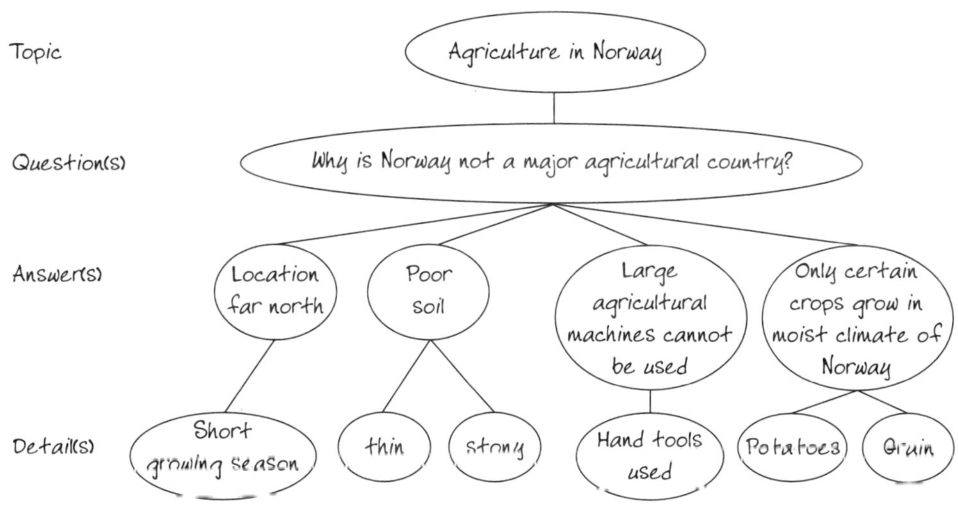

Create a question–answer graphic organizer for information you want to remember.

Learning about Graphic Organizers: Compare–Contrast

1-17

A **compare–contrast** graphic organizer shows how two things are alike and how they are different. Here are the questions you should answer to obtain the information needed to create a compare–contrast graphic organizer:

1. What two things are being compared and contrasted?
2. In what ways are the two things alike?
3. In what ways are the two things different?

Read the following class notes about the U.S. House of Representatives and the Senate. Then examine the compare–contrast graphic organizer for the notes.

> House of Representatives—National leaders elected for 2 yr term, members called representatives, leader called Speaker of House. Number of representatives based upon population. Represent their state. From all parties. Senate—National leaders, elected for 6 yr term, represent state, 2 senators per state. Leader called President of Senate. From all parties.

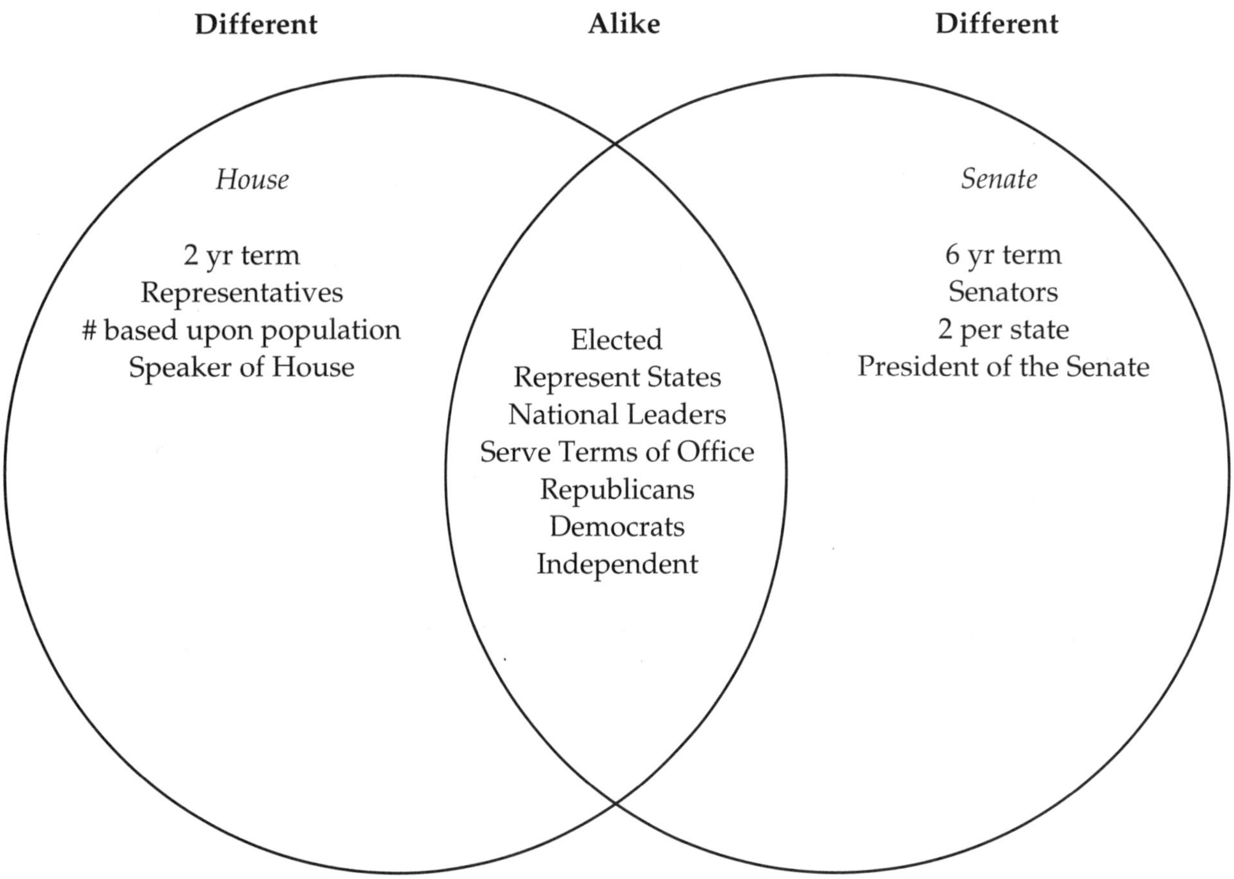

Create a compare–contrast graphic organizer for information you want to remember.

Learning about Graphic Organizers: Series of Events

1-18

A **series of events** graphic organizer shows a series of events in a logical order. Sometimes this pattern is used to describe the stages of something, such as the growth of a plant. At other times, the pattern is used to show the steps in a procedure, such as balancing a checkbook. The pattern also may be used to depict a sequence of events in time order, such as the events that led to the Persian Gulf War.

Here are the questions you should answer to obtain the information needed to create a series of events graphic organizer:

1. What is the topic?
2. What is the first stage, step, or event?
3. What are the intervening stages, steps, or events?
4. What is the final stage, step, or event?

Examine the series of events graphic organizer constructed from a psychology textbook showing Piaget's stages of cognitive development.

Topic	**Piaget's Stages of Cognitive Development**
First Stage	**Sensorimotor** Birth to 18–24 months Learn to represent the world internally Learn relationships between actions and external world Learn basic cause and effect
Intervening Stages	**Preoperational** 18–24 months to 7 years Growth of symbolic activity Language begins to develop Thought is egocentric Principle of conversation is acquired
	Concrete Operations 6–7 years to 11 years Logical thought emerges Problems can be solved Principle of reversibility is acquired
Final Stage	**Formal Operations** Age 12+ Deal with abstractions Adult thought emerges Hypothetico-deductive reasoning is used

Create a series of events graphic organizer for information you want to remember.

Learning about Graphic Organizers: Cause–Effect

1-19

A **cause–effect** graphic organizer is used to show how something occurs. Here are the questions you should answer to obtain the information needed to create a cause–effect graphic organizer:

1. What is the cause?
2. What is/are the effect(s)?
3. What details are associated with the effect(s)?

Read the following class notes about the importance of using techniques for remembering information. Then examine the cause–effect graphic organizer for the notes.

> It is important to use techniques to remember information you hear or read about in college. As a result of using remembering techniques, you can expect a number of good things to happen. You will remember more information. You will do better on tests, which will result in higher grades and scholarships. You will also feel better about yourself as a student. Finally, you will have greater career opportunities.

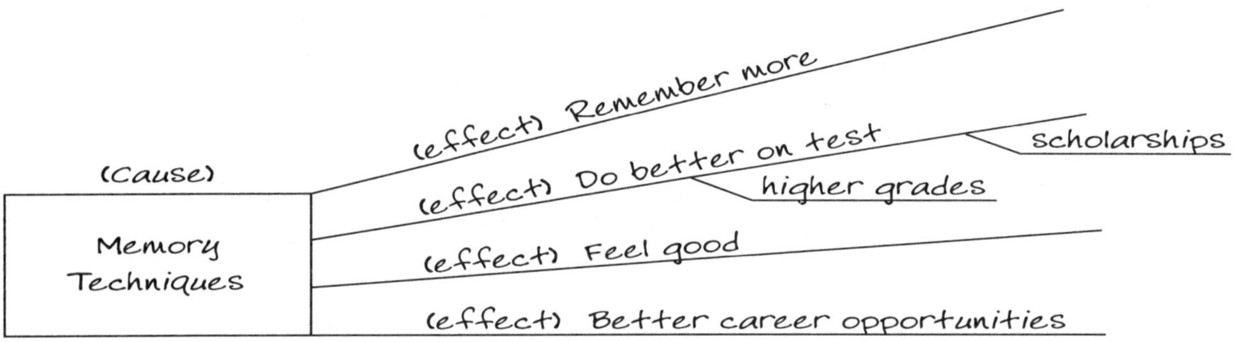

Create a cause–effect graphic organizer for information you want to remember.

Learning about Graphic Organizers: Problem–Solution

A **problem–solution** graphic organizer is used to show a problem, to demonstrate why it is a problem, to show attempts to solve the problem, and to show the solution or the status of the attempts. Here are the questions you should answer to obtain the information needed to create a problem–solution graphic organizer:

1. What is the problem?
2. Why is it a problem?
3. What attempts have been made to solve the problem?
4. What is the solution or status of these attempts?

Examine the problem–solution graphic organizer constructed from an economics textbook showing the U.S. national debt as a problem, why it is a problem, attempts to solve the problem, including details as necessary, and the solution or status of attempted solutions at a specific point in time. In this case, the attempts to solve the problem did not work. In other cases, the problem may be solved.

Problem:	U.S. national debt is too high.
	↓
Why?	Government cannot pay for goods and services.
	↓
Attempted Solutions and Details	Raise taxes. Reduce spending. Gramm–Rudman–Hollings Act Set annual budget decrement goals. Exempted certain programs from program cuts. Made automatic budget cuts across nonexempted programs.
	↓
Solution or Status	National debt remained at a high level.

Create a problem–solution graphic organizer for information you want to remember.

ANSWER KEY

1-1 1. Mnemonics. 2. Repetition. 3. Graphic organizers.

1-2 Repetition should be used for 1, 3, 5, 6.

1-3 1. SAULC. 2. Possibilities: CLAUS, LUCAS. 3. Possibilities: PIGMY, GIMPY. 4. Possibilities: BATBIM, BIMBAT.

1-4 Responses will vary.

1-5 1. N=Nixon, F=Ford, C=Carter, R=Reagan, B=Bush, C=Clinton. 2. Responses will vary. 3. TMSSNO.

1-6 through **1-14** Responses will vary.

1-15 through **1-20** Graphic organizers will vary.

CHAPTER TWO

Reading and Taking Notes from Textbooks Using SQ4R

OBJECTIVES

1. **Teach students about the SQ4R strategy.**
2. **Have students apply the SQ4R strategy to textbooks used in their classes.**

REPRODUCIBLE ACTIVITIES

2-1 Learning about SQ4R
2-2 Learning How to Use SQ4R
2-3 Practice Using SQ4R
2-4 Applying SQ4R
Answer Key

USING REPRODUCIBLE ACTIVITIES

Here is a plan for using the chapter reproducible activities. Activities may be completed by students either independently or in class.

1. Use 2-1 and 2-2 to introduce and demonstrate SQ4R.
2. Use 2-3 to provide practice using SQ4R.
3. Use 2-4 to have students apply SQ4R to a textbook they are using in one of their classes.

SQ4R

SQ4R is a textbook reading and notetaking strategy that will improve your reading comprehension, help you create a set of study notes, and extend the length of time you remember what you read. Each symbol in the strategy stands for one thing you must do. The abbreviation SQ4R will help you remember the steps in this textbook-reading and notetaking strategy. Here are the steps in SQ4R:

Survey
Question
Read
wRite
Remember
Review

Here is what you do for each step

Survey In this step you activate your prior knowledge and become familiar with the content of a textbook chapter you are about to read. This is what you must do to survey a chapter before you actually read it:

- Read the *title* to anticipate what the chapter is about.
- Read the *introduction,* which is found at the beginning of the chapter. Use the introduction to get a general idea about the chapter.
- Read the *side headings* to get specific ideas about the chapter.
- Examine any *visuals* and read their captions to add to your ideas about the chapter.
- If there is a *summary* or *conclusion,* read it to confirm your ideas about the chapter. The summary or conclusion is found at the end of the chapter.

Question In this step, formulate questions to think about and answer as you are reading. Searching for the answers to these questions will help you concentrate on what you are reading. Students who read without a clear purpose in mind frequently become inactive readers. Their eyes move across the lines from page to page, but their minds record nothing. Has this ever happened to you?

Formulate a question for each side heading. Questions can be formulated by placing **who, what, where, when, why,** or **how** in front of any side headings. Sometimes a side heading has many parts, and you might need to formulate a question about each part. Write each question in your notebook immediately after you formulate it.

Read In this step you read to get the information you need to answer the questions you formulated. Skim, read, and/or reread material to answer each question. Sometimes you will discover that a question you formulated does not match the information in the text. When this occurs, change your question to match the information presented in the text.

wRite In this step you write the answers to the questions you formulated. Answers should be written using as few words as possible. Your written questions and answers become **textbook notes** you use later to prepare for tests.

Remember Use what you learned about remembering information from Chapter One to remember the information in your textbook notes. If the information is not very detailed, use the repetition procedure to remember the information. If the information is detailed, use one of the mnemonic techniques to remember the information. If the information is very detailed, construct a graphic organizer to remember the information.

Review Periodically review the information using the remembering techniques. This will keep the information in your long-term memory.

Learning How to Use SQ4R

2-2

Look at the section titled "A Visit to Ancient Rome" from a textbook called *Early Civilization*. The chapter has been shortened for purposes of this activity. For demonstration purposes, the title, introduction, side headings, and conclusion are labeled. This is how a hypothetical student applied SQ4R to "A Visit to Ancient Rome."

Survey: The student read the title, introduction, side headings, and conclusion.

Question: The student read the first side heading and formulated a question. Both the side heading and question were written in the textbook notes that follow the reading selection. The student repeated the procedure for each side heading. Notice that for two of the side headings, the student wrote two questions.

Read: The student read the chapter to learn the answer to the first question.

wRite: The answer was written in the textbook notes. The Read and wRite steps were repeated for each question.

Remember: For each answer, the student decided to use repetition, a mnemonic technique, or a graphic organizer to remember the information.

Review: The student periodically reviewed the information.

Title–

A Visit to Ancient Rome

Introduction–

What do you think living in Rome was like a thousand or more years ago? It was quite exciting for the times because Rome was the cultural center of the known world. By taking a visit to ancient Rome, you will obtain a feeling for this marvelous city.

Side Heading–

ROMAN DRESS

The first thing a traveler to ancient Rome would see would be some male citizens going about their daily business dressed in long, woolen shirts called tunics. Those men who were involved in more formal routines would be wearing undyed wool togas over their tunics. In most weather all Romans wore strap sandals. The ladies of the city dressed in long stolas, tunics belted at the waist, worn over an inner tunic. They might wear a rectangular cloak if the weather was cold. Roman women often carried parasols and fans in hot weather. All the citizens dressed as comfortably as they could.

Side Heading–

FORMS OF ENTERTAINMENT

As he toured the city, the newcomer might wonder what forms of entertainment amused the citizens. He would probably hear shouts and cheers coming from an area where spectators were enjoying a circus, a play, or gladiatorial combat. These events took place often and lasted from sunrise to sundown. Admission was free so anyone who chose to could attend.

Another popular leisure time activity in ancient Rome was public bathing. Bathing establishments were quite elaborate. One would find games, lectures, and musical performances presented there. There were areas where people could lounge and gossip if they were not enjoying the baths. At the center of everything were the baths themselves, a cold bath, a warm bath, and a steam bath which bathers passed through in order. The baths were actually a large complex of business and entertainment areas.

Side Heading–

LIMITATIONS OF THE CITY

The tourist would be impressed with the Roman's love of grandeur as evidenced by the beauty of baths, but if he walked around the city long enough, he would become aware of the limitations it had. It would soon be obvious that as a visitor he would have to ask directions in order to get around. Most of the residential streets did not have names and the houses

LIVING LONG AGO 101

did not have numbers. There were few sidewalks and the streets were narrow and crowded. The tourist would have to be alert when he strolled down a residential street because at that time people disposed of their trash the easiest way, by throwing it out the window! Thus, walking around Rome was not only confusing, it was also dangerous.

Side Heading –

ROME AT NIGHT

Anyone visiting Rome would be well advised to do his sightseeing during the day because a walk through Rome at night was a dangerous adventure. There were no street lights to illuminate the heavy traffic that clogged the streets. During the day law prohibited chariots and tradesmen's carts from filling the streets of the city, so there was a great deal of traffic at night. There was also a lot of crime in the dark, crowded streets. Smart Romans stayed at home after sunset.

Side Heading –

HAZARDS OF TRAVEL

When the visitor to Rome decided to leave, he would have to choose his route home carefully. Travel outside the city was dangerous and difficult. Wealthy people traveled by carriage, usually accompanied by their household slaves and servants. Travelers would not stop at the inns and hotels along the way because they were apt to be dirty. They also tended to be the hangouts of robbers. Instead the Roman traveler would sleep in his carriage or in a tent put up by the side of the road. If the traveler was fortunate and had a friend who lived along the route, he could stay with him. There was an elaborate social system of *hospitium* or "guest friendship" that was similar to membership in a lodge. People were obligated to give those who were their friends protection and hospitality while they were on the road. Romans had to plan their journey well if they were to arrive at their destination safely.

Conclusion – You can see that living in the ancient city of Rome was both adventurous and dangerous. Life was very different from what we experience in the twentieth century. Dress, entertainment, travel, and conditions of living are much better today.

102 LIVING LONG AGO

TEXTBOOK NOTES

Chapter Title: A Visit to Ancient Rome

Textbook: *Early Civilizations*

1. *Side Heading:* ROMAN DRESS

   Question: How did men dress?
   Answer: Comfortably. Sandals. Tunics and sometimes togas.

   Question: How did women dress?
   Answer: Also comfortably: stolas, cloaks, and sandals.

2. *Side Heading:* FORMS OF ENTERTAINMENT

   Question: What did the Romans do for fun?
   Answer: Circuses, plays, gladiators, and public baths.

3. Side Heading: LIMITATIONS OF THE CITY

   Question: What were some of the problems Romans encountered living in Rome?
   Answer: Easy to get lost, narrow sidewalks. Hit by garbage from windows.

4. *Side Heading:* ROME AT NIGHT

   Question: What was Rome like at night?
   Answer: Dangerous! Inadequate light, high traffic and crime.

5. *Side Heading:* HAZARDS OF TRAVEL

   Question: Why was it dangerous to travel?
   Answer: Unclean inns. Robberies.

   Question: What was meant by *hospitium*?
   Answer: System of guest friendship much like today's lodge. People had to help friends who were traveling.

Here is a chapter from a college textbook on American government. Apply what you have learned about SQ4R to this textbook chapter. Write your questions and answers on the Textbook Notes form provided at the end of the textbook chapter.

Chapter 7
The Presidency

The Framers of the Constitution had little difficulty in agreeing that executive authority should be vested in one person, although some delegates suggested multiple executives to diffuse the power of the executive branch. The Framers also had no problem in agreeing on a title for the new office. Borrowing from the constitutions of Pennsylvania, Delaware, New Jersey, and New Hampshire, the Framers called the new chief executive the "president." How and by whom the president was to be chosen was a major stumbling block. The Virginia delegation proposed a "Virginia Plan" which called for a single national executive, elected by the national legislature, who would be ineligible for a second term. Reflecting the limited powers given to the Virginia governor by the state constitution, Virginia's delegates proposed an executive strictly accountable to the legislature.

QUALIFICATIONS FOR OFFICE

The Constitution requires that the president (and the vice president, whose major function is to succeed the president in the event of his death or disability) be a natural-born citizen of the United States, at least thirty-five years old, and a resident of the United States for at least fourteen years. In the 1700s it was not uncommon for those engaged in international diplomacy to be out of the country for substantial periods of time. Thus, the Framers wanted to make sure that prospective presidents spent some time in this country before running for its highest elective office.

TERM OF OFFICE

Initially, the length of the executive's term of office was the subject of considerable controversy. Four-, seven-, and eleven-year terms with no eligibility for reelection were suggested by various delegates to the Constitutional Convention. Alexander Hamilton suggested that a president serve during "good behavior." Not surprisingly, the issue of term length quickly became associated

Adapted with permission from *American Government: Roots and Reform* by K. O'Connor and L. J. Sabato, pp. 259–263, 265–271, 273, 303. Boston: Allyn and Bacon, 1995.

with eligibility to seek reelection. From the beginning, it was clear that if the delegates agreed to allow the *state* legislatures to choose the president, then shorter terms with the possibility of reelection would be favored. If they agreed to allow the national legislature to select the president, there would be no possibility for reelection. After the Framers of the Constitution reached agreement on the selection process, the delegates in favor of a reelection option prevailed, and a four-year term with eligibility for reelection was added to the proposed Article II of the Constitution.

The first president, George Washington (1789–1797), sought reelection only once, and a two-term limit for presidents became traditional. Although Ulysses S. Grant unsuccessfully sought a third term, the two terms established by Washington remained the standard for 150 years, avoiding the Framers' much-feared "constitutional monarch," a perpetually reelected tyrant. In the 1930s and 1940s, however, Franklin D. Roosevelt ran successfully in four elections as Americans fought first the Great Depression and then World War II. Despite Roosevelt's popularity, negative reaction to his long tenure in office ultimately led to passage (and ratification in 1951) of the Twenty-Second Amendment, which limits presidents to two four-year terms or a total of ten years in office, should a vice president assume a portion of a president's remaining term.

REMOVAL

During the Constitutional Convention, Benjamin Franklin, a staunch supporter of impeachment, a process for removing an official from office, noted that "historically, the lack of power to impeach had necessitated recourse to

Not everyone was enthusiastic about FDR's unprecedented attempt for a third term.

assassination."[1] Not surprisingly, he urged the rest of the delegates to formulate a legal mechanism for removing the president and vice president.

Just as the presidential veto power was a check on Congress, the impeachment provision ultimately included in Article II was adopted as a check on the power of the president (as well as the judiciary). Each house of Congress was given a role to play to assure that the chief executive could be removed only for "Treason, Bribery, or other high Crimes and Misdemeanors."

The Constitution gives the House of Representatives the power to conduct a thorough investigation to determine (in a manner similar to a grand jury proceeding) whether the president had engaged in any impeachable offenses. If the finding is affirmative, the House is empowered to vote to impeach the president by a simple majority. The precise charges against the president are called **articles of impeachment**, which are similar to a grand jury indictment. The Senate then acts as a court of law and tries the president for the charged offenses. The Chief Justice of the United States Supreme Court presides over the vote on the articles and the Senate hearing. A two-thirds majority vote in the Senate on any count contained in the articles of impeachment is necessary to remove the president from office. Only one president, Andrew Johnson in 1868, has ever been impeached, but the Senate vote fell one vote short of forcing his removal.

SUCCESSION

Through 1994, eight presidents have died in office, through illness or assassination. William Henry Harrison was the first president to die in office—he caught a cold at his inauguration in 1841 and died one month later. John Tyler thus became the first vice president to succeed to the presidency. In 1865, Abraham Lincoln became the first president to be assassinated. And in 1974, Richard M. Nixon, facing impeachment and likely conviction, became the first president to resign from office.

Whether the president has died or resigned, the vice president has always taken over the reins of office. The Constitution directs Congress to select a successor if the office of vice president is vacant. To clarify this provision, Congress passed the Presidential Succession Act of 1947, which lists in order those in line (after the vice president) to succeed the president:

1. Speaker of the House of Representatives
2. President pro tempore of the Senate
3. Secretaries of State, Treasury, and Defense, and other Cabinet heads in order of the creation of their department

[1]Winston Solberg, *The Federal Convention and the Formation of the Union of the American States* (Indianapolis: Bobbs-Merrill, 1958), p. 235.

The Succession Act has never been used because there has always been a vice president to take over. The Twenty-Fifth Amendment, in fact, was added to the Constitution in 1967 to assure that this will continue to be the case. Should a vacancy occur in the office of vice president, the Twenty-Fifth Amendment directs the president to appoint a new vice president, subject to the approval (by a simple majority) of both houses of Congress.

The Twenty-Fifth Amendment has been used twice in its relatively short history. In 1973, President Richard M. Nixon selected the House Minority Leader, Gerald R. Ford, to replace Vice President Spiro T. Agnew, after Agnew resigned in the wake of charges that he had accepted bribes while a local public official in Maryland and while vice president. Less than a year later, when Vice President Ford became the thirty-eighth president after Nixon's resignation after the **Watergate** scandal, he appointed (and the Senate approved) former four-term New York State Governor Nelson A. Rockefeller to the vice presidency. This set up, for the first time in U.S. history, a situation in which neither the president nor the vice president had been elected to those positions.

THE VICE PRESIDENT

The Framers gave little attention to the office of vice president beyond the need to have an immediate official "stand in" for the president. Initially, the vice president's only function was to assume the office of president in the case of the death of the president or some other emergency. After further debate, the delegates made the vice president the presiding officer of the Senate (except in cases of presidential impeachment). They feared that if the Senate's presiding officer were chosen from the Senate itself, one state would be short a representative. The vice president was given the authority to vote only in the event of a tie, however.

With so little authority, the office of vice president was considered until recently a sure place for a public official to disappear into obscurity. When John Adams wrote to his wife, Abigail, about his position as America's first vice president, he said it was "the most insignificant office that was the invention of man . . . or his imagination conceived."[2] A similar sentiment is evident in a story told by Thomas R. Marshall, Woodrow Wilson's little-remembered vice president: "Once there were two brothers. One ran away to sea. The other was elected vice president, and nothing was heard of either of them again."[3] Franklin D. Roosevelt's first vice president, John Nance Garner, more bluntly observed that his job was not worth "a pitcher of warm spit."

[2]Alfred Steinberg, *The First Ten: The Founding Presidents and Their Administrations* (New York: Doubleday, 1967), p. 59.

[3]As a presiding officer in the Senate, Marshall helped break the monotony of a lengthy speech on "What This Country Needs" by quipping his oft-repeated words: "What this country needs is a really good five-cent cigar." All comments noted in Carol Haas, *In the World of Politics* (Hauppauge, NY: Barron's Educational Services, 1991), p. 223.

Power and fame generally come only to those vice presidents who become president. Just "one heartbeat away" from the presidency, the vice president serves as a constant reminder of the president's mortality. In part, this situation has given rise to a trend of uneasy relationships between presidents and vice presidents, beginning as early as Adams and Jefferson. As historian Arthur M. Schlesinger, Jr., once noted, "The Vice President has only one serious thing to do: that is, to wait around for the President to die. This is hardly the basis for a cordial and enduring friendship."[4]

In the past, presidents chose their vice presidents largely to "balance"—politically, geographically, or otherwise—the presidential ticket, with little thought given to the possibility of the vice president becoming president. Franklin D. Roosevelt, for example, a liberal New Yorker, selected Garner, a conservative Texan, to be his running mate in 1932.

In general, presidential candidates since Eisenhower have selected running mates of such a caliber that they might eventually take over the reins of the nation's highest office. Since Jimmy Carter, recent presidents have given their vice presidents more and more responsibility as well as access to information vital to the country's national security. Thus, the office of vice president has begun to come into its own after years of ridicule and insignificance. Today, it is viewed as a jumping-off point for higher office, and not as a dead-end position, as more and more vice presidents have become president. Since 1952, the only elected vice president* who has not received his party's nod to run for president was Alben W. Barkley, who served under President Truman. Of the six vice presidents who have run for president since 1960, three have been elected: Lyndon B. Johnson, Richard M. Nixon, and George Bush. Hubert Humphrey, Gerald R. Ford, and Walter F. Mondale ran but lost. Dan Quayle is considered to be a possible candidate for the Republican nomination for president in 1996. Vice President Al Gore, Jr., too, is likely to be presidential candidate in the future, since he sought his party's nomination (unsuccessfully) in 1988.[5]

How much power a vice president has, however, depends upon how much the president is willing to give him. Although Jimmy Carter, a Southerner, chose Walter F. Mondale, a Northerner, as his running mate in 1976 to balance the ticket, he was also the first president to give his vice president more than ceremonial duties. Mondale—a former senator from Minnesota with Washington connections—became an important adviser to President Carter, who had run for office as a Washington "outsider." Whereas previous vice presidents had tried to make numerous trivial tasks appear significant, Mondale did his best to carve out a new role as an adviser to the president, an activity encouraged by Carter.

[4]"Is the Vice Presidency Necessary?" *Atlantic* 233 (May 1974): 37.

*Spiro Agnew was forced to resign from office.

[5]See Jules Whitcover, *Crapshoot: Rolling the Dice on the Vice Presidency* (New York: Crown, 1992).

The "Mondale model" of an active vice president set the expectations for what the influence, powers, and limitations of modern vice presidents should be. President Ronald Reagan's vice president, George Bush, a former director of the Central Intelligence Agency (CIA), was given the unprecedented responsibility of heading the National Security Crisis Management team. Following the assassination attempt on President Reagan in March 1981, Vice President Bush worked closely with the recuperating president to keep the government in order. George Bush also made good use of Vice President Dan Quayle. Quayle was a key player in keeping conservatives happy, and he also chaired the Council on Competitiveness, an executive council created by Bush to review all federal regulations that could have an adverse effect on business.

President Clinton has expanded on the "Mondale model." Gore and Clinton forged a close working (and apparently personal) relationship when they traveled the country campaigning by bus in 1992. With many more personal characteristics in common than many president/vice president teams (they are both Southerners, young, religious, fathers of teenage girls, and married to strong, independent women, for example), Clinton made sure Gore was at his side when key appointments were made, and the two consult on a daily basis.

The Constitutional Powers of the President

Despite the Framers' faith in George Washington as their intended first president, it took considerable compromise to overcome their continued fear of a king. The specific powers of the executive branch that the Framers agreed upon are enumerated in Article II of the Constitution. Perhaps the most important section of Article II is its first sentence. It provides that "The executive Power shall be vested in a President of the United States of America." Just what the Framers meant by "executive power" was left intentionally vague.

Over the years, the expected limits of these constitutional powers have changed as individual presidents asserted themselves in the political process. Some presidents are powerful and effective, others just limp along in office. Much of the president's authority stems from his position as the symbolic leader of the nation and his ability to wield power. When the president speaks—especially in the area of foreign affairs—he speaks for the whole nation. But the base of all presidential authority is Article II, which outlines only a limited policy-making role for the president. Thus, as administrative head of the executive branch, the president is charged with taking "Care that the Laws be faithfully executed," but he has no actual power to make Congress enact legislation he supports.

THE APPOINTMENT POWER

To help him enforce the laws passed by Congress, the Constitution authorizes the president to appoint, with the advice and consent of the Senate,

> Ambassadors, other public Ministers and Consuls, judges of the supreme Court, and all other Officers of the United States, whose Appointments are not herein otherwise provided for, and which shall be established by Law. . . .

Today, with the growth of the Executive Office of the President—as well as of the Cabinet, executive agencies, and commissions—the president has accumulated the authority to make more than 3,000 appointments to his administration (technically more than 75,000, if military officers are included). Although only about half of these appointments are to policy-making positions, this power gives a president considerable influence over policy making. In the context of his ability to make appointments to the federal courts, especially, his influence can be felt far past his term of office.

The quality of presidential appointments directly reflects upon the president. Presidents Ulysses S. Grant, Warren G. Harding, and Richard M. Nixon, for example, were hurt by the low quality of some of their appointments. Likewise, President Ronald Reagan's reputation suffered when the behavior of several of his appointees led to numerous resignations and/or federal prosecutions of high-ranking appointees. And President Bill Clinton was widely criticized about the way some of his appointments were handled and for the fact that it took him so long to fill key positions. The Constitution is silent on the president's authority to remove those subject to senatorial appointment, but the Supreme Court has interpreted the Constitution to allow the president to remove most appointees at will.

THE POWER TO CONVENE CONGRESS

The Constitution requires the president to inform the Congress periodically on "the State of the Union," and authorizes the president to convene either or both houses of Congress on "extraordinary Occasions." In *Federalist No. 77*, Hamilton justified the latter by noting that because the Senate and the chief executive enjoy concurrent powers to make treaties, "it might often be necessary to call it together with a view to this object, when it would be unnecessary and improper to convene the House of Representatives."

THE POWER TO MAKE TREATIES

The president's power to make treaties with foreign nations is checked by the Constitution's stipulation that all treaties must be approved by at least two-thirds of the members of the Senate. The chief executive can also "receive ambassadors," wording that has been interpreted to allow the president to recognize the very existence of other nations.

Historically, the Senate ratifies about 70 percent of the treaties submitted to it by the president.[6] Only sixteen that have been put to a vote have been rejected, often under highly partisan circumstances. Perhaps the most notable example of the Senate's refusal to ratify a treaty was its defeat of the Treaty of Versailles submitted by President Woodrow Wilson. The Treaty was an agreement among the major nations to end World War I, and it called for, at Wilson's insistence, the creation of a League of Nations—a precursor of the United Nations—to foster continued peace and international disarmament. In struggling to gain international acceptance for the League, Wilson had taken American support for granted. This was a dramatic miscalculation. Isolationists, led by Senator William Jennings Bryan (D.-Neb.), opposed U.S. participation in the League on the grounds that the League would place the United States in the center of every major international conflict. Proponents countered that, League or no League, the United States had emerged from World War I as a world power, and that membership in the League would enhance its new role. The vote for ratification was very close, but the isolationists prevailed—the United States stayed out of the League, and Wilson was devastated.

The Senate may also require substantial amendment of a treaty prior to granting its consent. When President Carter proposed the controversial Panama Canal Treaties in 1977, for example, the Senate required that several conditions be ironed out between the Carter and Torrijos administrations before its approval was forthcoming.

Presidents often try to get around the "advise and consent" requirement of treaties by entering into an **executive agreement**, which allows the president to enter into secret and highly sensitive arrangements with foreign nations without congressional approval. Presidents have used these agreements since the days of George Washington, and their use has been upheld by the courts. Although executive agreements are not binding on subsequent administrations, since 1900 they have been used far more frequently than treaties, further cementing the role of the president in foreign affairs.

VETO POWER

Another way presidents can affect the policy process is through **veto** power, the authority to reject any congressional legislation. Proponents of a strong executive at the Constitutional Convention argued that the president should have an absolute and final veto over acts of Congress. Opponents of this idea, including Benjamin Franklin, countered that in their home states the executive veto "was constantly made use of to extort money" from the legislature.

[6]Benjamin I. Page and Mark P. Petracca, *The American Presidency* (New York: McGraw-Hill, 1983), p. 268.

James Madison made the most compelling argument for a compromise on the issue:

> Experience has proven a tendency in our governments to throw all power into the legislative vortex. The Executives of the States are in general little more than Ciphers, the legislatures omnipotent. If no effectual check be devised for restraining the instability and encroachments of the latter, a revolution of some kind or other would be inevitable.[7]

In keeping with the system of checks and balances, then, the president was given veto power but only as a "qualified negative." Although the president was given the authority to veto any act of Congress (with the exception of joint resolutions that propose constitutional amendments), Congress was given the authority to override an executive veto by a two-thirds vote in each House. The veto is a powerful policy tool because Congress cannot usually muster enough votes to override it. Thus, in over 200 years there have been approximately 2,500 presidential vetoes and only 100-odd have been overridden.

COMMANDER-IN-CHIEF OF THE MILITARY

One of the most important executive powers is the president's authority over the military. Article II states that the president is "Commander-in-Chief of the Army and Navy of the United States." The Framers saw this power as consistent with state practices, and since the eighteenth century it has proven to be wide-ranging. While the Constitution specifically grants Congress the authority to declare war, presidents since Abraham Lincoln have used the commander-in-chief clause in conjunction with the chief executive's duty to "take Care that the Laws be faithfully executed" to wage war (and to broaden various powers).

THE PARDONING POWER

Presidents can exercise a check on judicial power through their constitutional authority to grant reprieves or pardons. A **pardon**, which restores all rights and privileges of citizenship, is usually granted to a specific individual convicted of a crime. In 1974, President Gerald R. Ford granted the most famous presidential pardon, to former President Richard M. Nixon, who had not been formally charged with any crime, "for any offenses against the United States, which he, Richard M. Nixon, has committed or may have committed while in office." This unilateral pardon unleashed a torrent of public criticism that many blame for Ford's ultimate defeat in his 1976 bid for the presidency.

[7]Quoted in Solberg, *The Federal Convention and the Formation of the Union of American States*, p. 91.

SUMMARY

1. Distrust of a too-powerful leader led the Framers to create an executive office with limited powers. They mandated that a president be thirty-five years old and opted not to limit the president's term of office. To further guard against tyranny, they also made provisions for the removal of the president and created an office of vice president to provide for an orderly transfer of power.
2. The Framers gave the president a variety of specific constitutional powers in Article II, including the powers to make appointments, to convene Congress, to make treaties, and to veto. The president also derives considerable power from being Commander-in-Chief of the military. The Constitution also grants the president the power to grant pardons.

TEXTBOOK NOTES

Textbook: *American Government*
Chapter Title: The Presidency

1. *Side Heading:* QUALIFICATIONS FOR OFFICE
   Question(s):

   Answer(s):

2. *Side Heading:* TERM OF OFFICE
   Question(s):

   Answer(s):

3. *Side Heading:* REMOVAL
   Question(s):

   Answer(s):

4. *Side Heading:* SUCCESSION
   Question(s):

   Answer(s):

5. *Side Heading:* THE VICE PRESIDENT
Question(s):

Answer(s):

6. *Main Heading:* THE CONSTITUTIONAL POWERS OF THE PRESIDENT
Question(s):

Answer(s):

7. *Side Heading:* THE APPOINTMENT POWER
Question(s):

Answer(s):

8. *Side Heading:* THE POWER TO CONVENE CONGRESS
Question(s):

Answer(s):

9. *Side Heading:* THE POWER TO MAKE TREATIES
Question(s):

Answer(s):

10. *Side Heading:* VETO POWER
Question(s):

Answer(s):

11. *Side Heading:* COMMANDER-IN-CHIEF OF THE MILITARY
Question(s):

Answer(s):

12. *Side Heading:* THE PARDONING POWER
Question(s):

Answer(s):

Applying SQ4R

2-4

1. Write the word associated with each step in the SQ4R strategy. Next to each word, write what you must do for that step.

2. Now use SQ4R to read and take notes from a chapter in a textbook you are using in one of your courses. Write your questions and answers in your notebook using the Textbook Notes format.

ANSWER KEY

2-1 No response required.
2-2 No response required.
2-3 Possible questions (Q) and answers (A):

1. Q: What are the qualifications for becoming President?
   A: Natural-born U.S. citizen, at least 35 years old, and U.S. resident for at least 14 years.
2. Q: How long is the term of office?
   A: Limited to two four-year terms or a total of 10 years in office.
3. Q. What process is used to remove a president from office before a term expires?
   A: Impeachment.
   Q: What is the impeachment procedure?
   A: First the House has to vote by a simple majority to impeach the President. Then the Senate must vote for removal by a two-thirds majority vote.
4. Q: Who takes over when a president dies or resigns?
   A: The vice president.
   Q: Who are next in succession?
   A: Speaker of the House; president pro tempore of the Senate; secretaries of State, Treasury, and Defense; and other cabinet heads in order of the creation of their department.
5. Q: What is the role of the vice president?
   A: Presiding officer of the Senate.
   Q: How is the office of vice president viewed today?
   A: Jumping-off point for higher office.
6. Q: What are the constitutional powers of the president?
   A: Article II of the Constitution outlines a limited policymaking role. The president has no power to make Congress enact legislation.
7. Q: What appointment power does the president have?
   A: With the advice and consent of the Senate, the Constitution authorizes the president to appoint ambassadors, justices of the Supreme Court, and all other offices of the United States whose appointments are not otherwise established by law.
8. Q: Who has the power to convene Congress?
   A: The president.
9. Q: Who has the power to make treaties?
   A: The president, subject to the approval of the Senate.
10. Q: What is veto power?
    A: The authority to reject any congressional legislation.
    Q: Who holds this power?
    A: The president.
11. Q: Who is commander-in-chief of the military?
    A: The president.
12. Q: What is a pardon?
    A: The restoration of all rights and privileges of citizenship.
    Q: Who has the power to pardon?
    A: The president.

2-4 1. **S = Survey.** Read title, introduction, sideheadings, visuals, and summary or conclusion.
Q = Question. Formulate questions.
R = Read. Read to get the information needed to answer the questions.
R = wRite. Write answers for the questions.
R = Remember. Select repetition, mnemonic techniques, or graphic organizers to remember information.
R = Review. Review the information periodically.
2. Responses will vary.

CHAPTER THREE

Taking Notes in Class

OBJECTIVES

1. **Teach students the three stages of notetaking.**
2. **Teach students to write less without losing meaning.**
3. **Teach students to identify six lecture styles.**
4. **Teach students how to construct graphic organizers from their notes.**

REPRODUCIBLE ACTIVITIES

3-1 What I Do When Taking Notes
3-2 What You Should Do When Taking Notes
3-3 Writing Less without Losing Meaning
3-4 Forming Abbreviations for Words
3-5 Forming Abbreviations for Terms
3-6 Using Symbols
3-7 Getting to Know How Instructors Lecture
3-8 Topic–List Lecture Style
3-9 Topic–List Graphic Organizer
3-10 Question–Answer Lecture Style
3-11 Question–Answer Graphic Organizer
3-12 Compare–Contrast Lecture Style
3-13 Compare–Contrast Graphic Organizer
3-14 Series of Events Lecture Style
3-15 Series of Events Graphic Organizer
3-16 Cause–Effect Lecture Style
3-17 Cause–Effect Graphic Organizer
3-18 Problem–Solution Lecture Style
3-19 Problem–Solution Graphic Organizer
3-20 Identifying How Your Instructors Lecture
Answer Key

USING REPRODUCIBLE ACTIVITIES

Here is a plan for using the chapter reproducible activities. Activities may be completed by students either independently or in class.

1. Use 3-1 and 3-2 to teach students about the three stages of note taking.
2. Use 3-3 through 3-6 to teach students how to write less without losing meaning.
3. Use 3-7 to introduce students to the six lecture styles used by instructors.
4. Use 3-8 through 3-19 to teach students to identify the six lecture styles and to prepare graphic organizers for each style.
5. Use 3-20 to have students apply what they have learned by identifying the lecture styles used by their instructors.

What I Do When Taking Notes **3-1**

Many students think that taking notes in class is simply a matter of writing down what the instructor says. However, good notetakers use a three-stage strategy for taking notes. Complete the following self-assessment to show what you do for each stage.

Stage One. *Before* I take notes, I do the following:

Stage Two. *During* the time I take notes, I do the following:

Stage Three. *After* I take notes, I do the following to make them more useful for studying for tests:

What You Should Do When Taking Notes 3-2

Here are the things you should do in the **before**, **during**, and **after** stages of taking class notes. Make a check mark (✓) before each statement you included in your self-assessment.

Before

- Complete all assigned reading.
- Review notes from previous class.
- Anticipate your instructor's goal for the lecture.
- Have notetaking materials ready.

During

- Listen for your instructor's statement of the goal.
- Listen to identify your instructor's lecture pattern.
- Write only the words needed to record the ideas presented.
- When possible, use abbreviations and symbols as you write.
- Copy into your notes information that is presented visually.
- Place a ? next to anything you write but do not understand.
- Leave blanks for information missed.

After

- Ask your instructor to explain things you wrote in your notes but do not understand.
- Compare your notes with those of other students to make sure your notes are complete and accurate.
- Use the glossary or a dictionary to define unknown words and terms. Write the definitions in the margin.
- Rewrite your notes if they are difficult to read or follow.
- Use mnemonic techniques to help you remember the information in your notes.

The more statements you checked, the better your notetaking strategy.

Writing Less without Losing Meaning **3-3**

Instructors talk at a rate that is faster than you can write. Although you do not have to write down everything an instructor says to have good notes, you do have to write down the important ideas. Here are some ways you can write all the important ideas without writing every word you hear.

- Write only the words needed to capture the important ideas presented by your instructor.
- Use standard abbreviations (FL for Florida) or your own abbreviations (*info* for *information*) for words.
- Use standard symbols for words (& for *and*).

Read this statement from a lecture. Then answer the two questions.

> Today we will learn how the heart ensures that blood is constantly recirculated to parts of the body. The two upper chambers of the heart are called the atria or auricles. They are large collecting chambers that receive blood from the rest of the body. The two lower chambers are known as ventricles. It is from the ventricles that blood is pumped back into the body. Small valves regulate the steady, rhythmic flow of blood between chambers and prevent inappropriate backwash. This is how the four chambers of the heart work together.

1. How many words are in the statement?

2. How many letters are in the statement?

Now rewrite the statement using what you have learned about how to capture all the important ideas in a lecture without writing down every word you hear. Then answer the questions that follow.

3. How many words are in your rewritten statement?

4. Did you use any symbols? If yes, how many?

5. How many letters are in your rewritten statement?

6. What has this activity taught you about taking notes?

Forming Abbreviations for Words **3-4**

A good way to increase your notetaking speed is to use abbreviations. It is important to write abbreviations whose meaning you will later be able to recognize. Here are some common words and their standard abbreviations.

Word	*Abbreviation*	*Word*	*Abbreviation*
psychology	psy	medicine	med
English	Eng	diameter	dia
month	mo	year	yr
vocabulary	vocab	Illinois	IL

For words that do not have a standard abbreviation, you will have to create your own abbreviations. Here are two ways to do this:

1. Write down only the consonants: *wrkbk = workbook; stmch = stomach.*
2. Write down only the first three or four letters: *sec = secretary; bec = because.*

Write an abbreviation for each of the following. You can use standard abbreviations or create your own. Be sure you can recognize the words from the abbreviations you create.

September	revolution
chemistry	pound
national	bibliography
anatomy	chapter
general	street
manager	telephone
auditorium	lecture
science	kilogram
mathematics	hour
gallon	veterinarian
agency	page
product	Thursday

Forming Abbreviations for Terms **3-5**

Terms are groups of words with a particular meaning. Like words, terms can be abbreviated. Some terms have standard abbreviations. For example, USA is the standard abbreviation for the United States of America. Standard abbreviations for terms are usually formed by writing the first letter of each word in the term. The first letter of small words (*and*, *or*, *of*) is often omitted from the abbreviation. Write the standard abbreviation for each of the following terms:

1. Central Intelligence Agency

2. National Aeronautics and Space Administration

3. Eastern Standard Time

4. North Atlantic Treaty Organization

5. estimated time of arrival

The following terms do not have standard abbreviations. Create your own abbreviation for each term. Do this by writing only the consonants in each word, writing the first three or four letters of each word, or writing the first initial of each word.

6. high school principal

7. organic chemistry textbook

8. physical education instructor

9. longitude and latitude

10. historical factor

Using Symbols 3-6

Another way to write quickly is to use symbols for words or terms. Here are some common words and terms and their symbols.

Σ	sum	&	and	Ψ	psychology
@	at	#	number	$	money
=	equals, equal to	?	question	w/o	without
L	right angle	∴	therefore	∵	because
÷	divided by	≠	not equal to	\	difference
>	greater than	<	less than	| |	parallel
⊥	perpendicular	∠	angle	°	degree
′	minute	″	second	¢	cent

Use what you have learned about abbreviations and symbols to rewrite each sentence.

1. Gestalt psychologists believe that the sum of the parts is greater than the whole.

2. Thirty-eight percent of working single mothers have their young children cared for in someone else's home, while less than 5 percent care for their children at work.

3. The athlete completed the marathon in 2 hours, 25 minutes, 13 seconds.

4. The difference between parallel lines and perpendicular lines is that parallel lines go in the same direction whereas perpendicular lines intersect or form right angles.

Getting to Know How Instructors Lecture

3-7

To be a successful notetaker, you must be able to identify the lecture style used by your instructors. Read to learn how to identify the lecture style being used.

The **topic–list** lecture style is being used when your instructor:

1. begins by presenting a topic for the day's lecture.
2. follows by listing subtopics.
3. continues with a list of details that go with the subtopics.

The **question–answer** lecture style is being used when your instructor:

1. begins by presenting a topic for the day's lecture.
2. follows by presenting one or more questions.
3. continues by providing answers.
4. adds details as necessary.

The **compare–contrast** lecture style is being used when your instructor:

1. begins by identifying two things that will be compared and contrasted.
2. follows by giving examples of how the two things are alike and how they are different.

The **series of events** lecture style is being used when your instructor:

1. begins by identifying the topic.
2. then identifies an initial event, step, or stage.
3. follows by providing information about intervening events, steps, or stages.
4. concludes by describing the final event, step, or stage.

The **cause–effect** lecture style is being used when your instructor:

1. begins by presenting a cause.
2. follows by giving one or more effects.
3. continues by presenting details associated with the effect(s).

The **problem–solution** lecture style is being used when your instructor:

1. begins by presenting a problem.
2. follows by explaining why it is a problem.
3. continues by telling about attempts to solve the problem, providing details as necessary.
4. concludes by telling the solution or the status of the attempts.

Topic–List Lecture Style

3-8

Instructors organize their lectures in predictable styles. One of these styles is called **topic–list**. The instructor begins by presenting the topic for the lecture and the associated subtopics. Each subtopic may be followed by details. Number words like **one** or **first** and words like **next, another, then,** and **finally** are used by instructors to signal a change from one subtopic to another or one detail to another.

Read the following excerpt from a lecture to see how an instructor used the topic-list style.

> If everyone is ready, we'll get started. Today I want to focus on why we place people in prison. There are approximately 3 million people in America's jails at the local, state, and federal level. And the number is growing. There are four main reasons why we place people in prison. First, there is retribution. This means people are placed in prison as a way to have them repay their debt to society. Another reason is deterrence. It is thought that if people know they will have to go to prison for committing a crime, they will be less likely to commit a crime. This is why some experts maintain that sentences must be sufficiently long to serve as a powerful deterrent. Next is rehabilitation. Here one goal is to change the behavior of individuals so they become conforming members of society. Another goal of the rehabilitation model of imprisonment is to provide inmates with education and training so they will have the skills to support themselves without resorting to crime. Finally, there is incapacitation. This means criminals are kept away from others to whom they may be harmful. In other words, criminals are kept off the streets. Now let's talk about what you think is the best model. . . .

1. Write the topic for this lecture.

2. List the four subtopics. For each subtopic, list the details, if any. For each detail, list the subdetails, if any.
   a.

   b.

   c.

   d.

3. What words were used to signal a change from one subtopic to another or from one detail to another?

Topic–List Graphic Organizer

3-9

A graphic organizer will help you better understand and remember the information presented in a lecture. There is a graphic organizer for each lecture style described in 3-7. Here is a graphic organizer that can be used to show how ideas are related for a topic–list lecture style.

1. Use the information from the lecture in 3-8 to complete the graphic organizer.

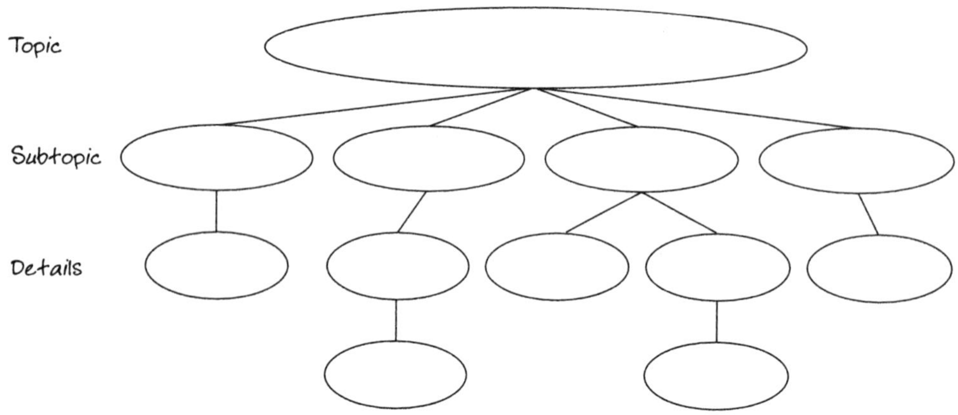

2. Use the graphic organizer to write a summary of the lecture that contains only a few sentences and is in your own words. Check to see if your summary captured the important information from the lecture.

Question–Answer Lecture Style

3-10

Sometimes instructors organize lectures using a style called **question–answer**. An instructor who uses this style begins by introducing a topic, followed by one or more questions. Each question is then answered. Details are sometimes included with an answer. **Who**, **what**, **where**, **when**, **why**, **how**, and **in what way(s)** are signals that a question–answer lecture style is being used.

Read the following excerpt from a lecture to see how one instructor used the question–answer style.

> Hi folks! Today I want to talk about a new American phenomenon, the commuter marriage.
>
> Does anyone know what a commuter marriage is?
>
> It's a marriage in which the husband and wife work in different geographical locations. The husband might work in Washington, D.C., and the wife in Philadelphia.
>
> They live together on the weekends in Fairfax, Virginia.
>
> What are these marriages like?
>
> They are often lonely. Both spouses live alone for much of the year in their own apartments. Often they know little about the people living near them.
>
> It is often hectic being in a commuter marriage. What other couples do over the course of a week they must accomplish in a weekend. This produces tension, which often leads to arguments.
>
> It is difficult to raise a family. The responsibility for feeding, clothing, and counseling children falls more heavily on one partner.
>
> We are likely to have more commuter marriages. Why?
>
> Well, most sociologists believe there will be more because women are increasingly pursuing careers that take them to places other than where their husbands work.

1. What words signal the use of the question–answer style?

2. Write the topic for this lecture.

3. Write the three questions used by the instructor to organize the lecture. For each, write the answer and any supporting details provided for the answer.

   a.

   b.

   c.

Question–Answer Graphic Organizer **3-11**

Here is a graphic organizer that can be used to show how ideas are related when a question–answer lecture style is used.

1. Use the information from the lecture in 3-10 to complete the graphic organizer.

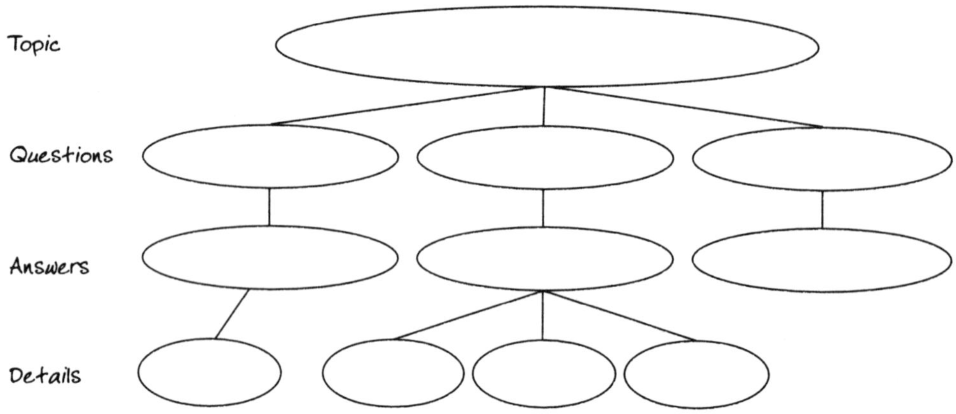

2. Use the graphic organizer to write a summary of the lecture in your own words that contains only a few sentences. Check to see if your summary captured the important information from the lecture.

Compare–Contrast Lecture Style

3-12

Sometimes instructors organize lectures using a style called **compare–contrast**. When this style is used, the instructor begins by identifying two things that will be compared and contrasted. The instructor then tells how the two things are alike and how they are different.

Certain words and phrases signal that a compare–contrast lecture style is being used. For example, **compare, like, similarly, correspondingly, in parallel, counterpart, equal to,** and **resemble** signal similarities. Words or phrases such as **differently, in contrast, however, difference between, antithesis of, disparity, distinction, in comparison, on the one hand, on the other hand, opposite,** and **on the contrary** signal differences.

Read the following excerpt from a lecture to see how an instructor used the compare–contrast style.

> Politicians are always interested in the opinions of their constituents. Opinions can be obtained by using what are called polls. Polls are surveys of the public to obtain information regarding how people think about some issue. Telephone polls and in-person polls are used to get information. They are alike in some ways and distinct in others. In a telephone poll, the pollster obtains information by calling people. This is the least expensive way to poll people. Very often a computer is used to select telephone numbers at random to be dialed. In an in-person poll, the pollster actually meets face to face with the person being polled. Research has shown that how the pollster dresses or looks can affect responses. Just as in a telephone poll, tone of voice can affect results. Regardless of the type of poll used, it is important that the sample represent the population.

1. What words were used to signal the compare–contrast style?

2. What is being compared and contrasted?

3. What are the similarities?

4. What are the differences?

Compare–Contrast Graphic Organizer **3-13**

Here is a graphic organizer that can be used to show how ideas are related when a compare–contrast lecture style is used.

1. Use the information from the lecture in 3-12 to complete the graphic organizer.

Different **Alike** **Different**

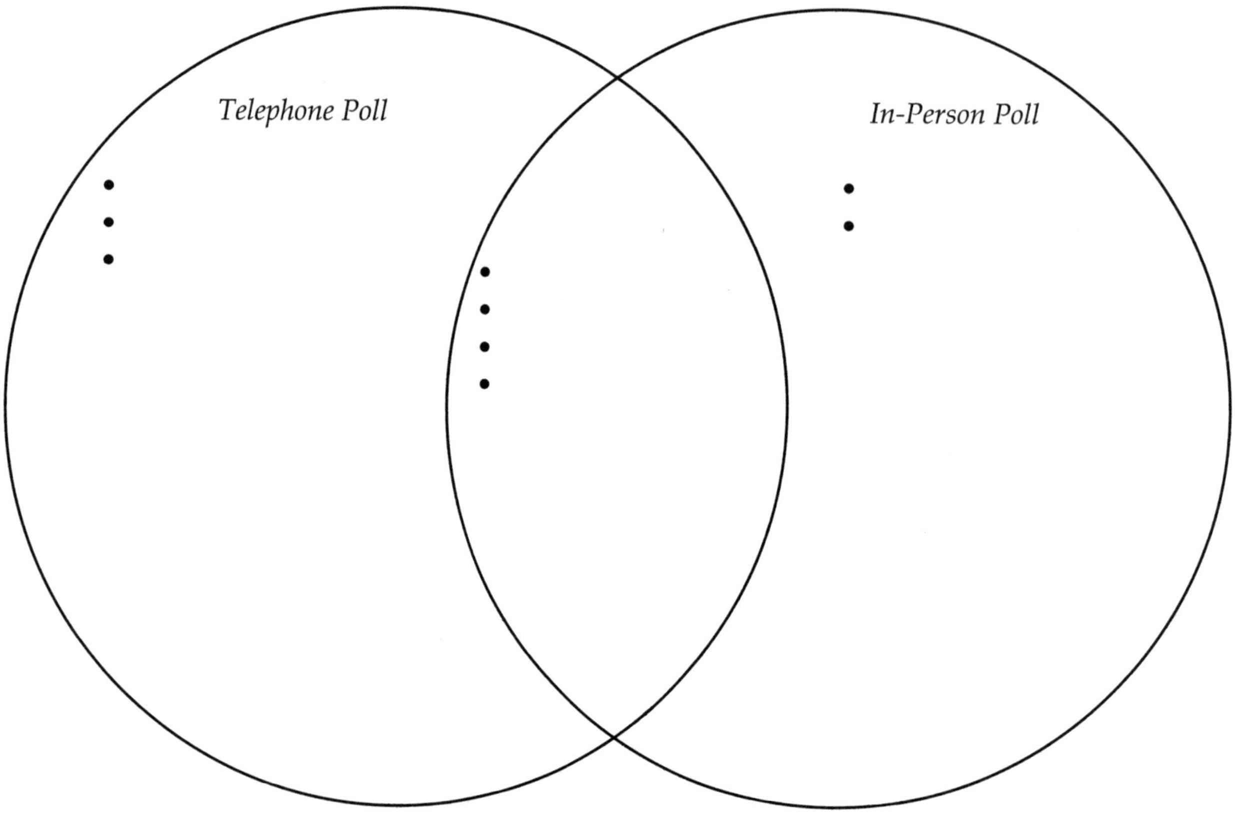

2. Use the graphic organizer to write a summary of the lecture in your own words that contains only a few sentences. Check to see if your summary captured the important information from the lecture.

Series of Events Lecture Style

Sometimes instructors organize their lectures using a style called **series of events**. When this style is used, the instructor begins by identifying the topic. Then the instructor presents the initial event, step, or stage, followed by information about intervening events, steps, or stages. The lecture is concluded when the instructor describes the final event, step, or stage. Words or phrases like **first**, **initially**, **at the outset**, **second**, **next**, **followed by**, **then**, **later**, **after**, **succeeding**, **intermediate**, **last**, **culminating**, and **finally** signal that a series of events lecture style is being used.

Read the following excerpt from a lecture to see how an instructor used the series of events style.

> A number of landmark events led to the Declaration of Independence by the settlers in the American colonies in 1776. Let me tell you about a few of them. First was the Mayflower Compact of 1620, which contained a set of minimal rules by which colonists in Massachusetts Bay could live their lives. The second was the Sugar Act of 1764, which placed taxes on sugar, wine, coffee, and other products exported to the colonies. This was followed the next year by the Stamp Act of 1765, which required the purchase of stamps for all documents such as newspapers and commercial papers. Next, in 1767, the British government enacted the Townshend Acts, which imposed duties on all kinds of colonial imports. This was followed by the assembling of the First Continental Congress in 1774. This group drafted the Declaration of Rights and Resolves, portions of which became part of the Declaration of Independence. Finally on July 4, 1776, the Second Continental Congress voted to adopt the Declaration of Independence written by Thomas Jefferson.

1. What words were used to signal the series of events style?

2. What is the topic?

3. In order, list the events. Add details as necessary.

Series of Events Graphic Organizer **3-15**

Here is a graphic organizer that can be used to show how ideas are related when a series of events lecture style is used.

1. Use the information from the lecture in 3-14 to complete the graphic organizer.

Topic ____

First Event	
	↓
Intervening Events	
	↓
Final Event	

2. Use the graphic organizer to write a summary of the lecture in your own words that contains only a few sentences. Check to see if your summary captured the important information from the lecture.

Cause–Effect Lecture Style

Sometimes instructors organize their lectures using a style called **cause–effect**. When this style is used, the instructor begins by presenting a cause of something, followed by one or more effects that go with the cause. Words or phrases like **since**, **thus**, **therefore**, **because**, **consequently**, **accordingly**, **so**, **hence**, **for that reason**, **inasmuch as**, **on account of**, **owing to**, **due to**, **whereas**, and **as a result** signal that a cause–effect lecture style is being used.

Read the following excerpt from a lecture to see how an instructor used the cause–effect style.

> Because of the high incidence of death and injury from front-end impact in automobile accidents, manufacturers are installing driver side air bags in their vehicles. Some manufacturers are beginning to place air bags on the passenger side as well. Engines are now mounted so that upon impact they move downward rather than into the passenger compartment. Manufacturers are also strengthening automobile frames to better withstand impacts. They are doing so by placing extra metal supports in the door frames. Beyond these structural changes, manufacturers have sponsored consumer education programs to promote safe driving habits. Some of these programs are directed toward adults, while others are designed for teenage drivers.

1. What word was used to signal the cause–effect style?

2. Write the cause statement.

3. List the effects and their details.

Cause–Effect Graphic Organizer

Here is a graphic organizer that can be used to show how ideas are related when a cause–effect style is used.

1. Use the information from the lecture in 3-16 to complete the graphic organizer.

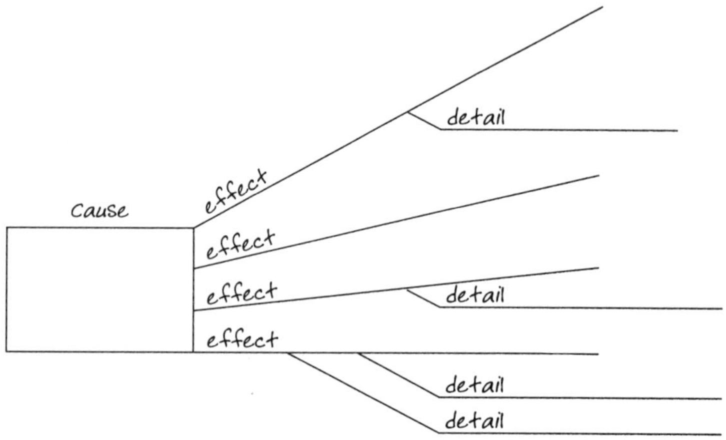

2. Use the graphic organizer to write a summary of the lecture in your own words that contains only a few sentences. Check to see if your summary captured the important information from the lecture.

Problem–Solution Lecture Style

Sometimes instructors organize their lectures using a style called **problem–solution**. When this style is used, the instructor begins by presenting a problem and explaining why it is a problem. The instructor continues by telling about attempts to solve the problem, providing details as necessary. The instructor concludes by identifying the solution or status of the attempts to solve the problem.

The following words or phrases signal that a problem–solution lecture style is being used. Words or phrases like **problem**, **point of dispute**, **subject of dispute**, **puzzle**, **conundrum**, **enigma**, **issue**, **bafflement**, **tough nut to crack**, and **complication** signal that a problem is being presented. Words or phrases like **solution**, **solve**, **answer**, **explanation**, **explication**, **interpretation**, **resolve**, **elucidate**, **clear up**, **unravel**, **work out**, and **untangle** signal that a solution is being proposed.

Read the following excerpt from a lecture to see how an instructor used the problem–solution style.

> Coronary heart disease is a problem throughout the world. This dreaded disease is killing many people. Coronary heart disease is a condition that occurs when arteries become clogged and no longer allow the necessary amount of blood to pass through to the heart. To solve this problem, doctors recommend that we eat less meat. Meat contains too much fat and cholesterol. Doctors also recommend that people stop using tobacco products. Smoking constricts blood vessels and raises blood pressure. Americans need more activity in their lifestyle too. Reducing weight to ideal body weight reduces the risk of heart disease. Until people implement these recommendations, coronary heart disease will remain a major killer.

1. What words signal the use of the problem–solution style?

2. Write the problem statement.

3. List the solutions and their details.

Problem–Solution Graphic Organizer **3-19**

Here is a graphic organizer that can be used to show how ideas are related when a problem–solution lecture style is used.

1. Use the information from the lecture in 3-18 to complete the graphic organizer.

Problem

↓

Why?

↓

Attempted Solutions and Details

↓

Solution or Status

2. Use the graphic organizer to write a summary of the lecture in your own words that contains only a few sentences. Check to see if your summary captured the important information from the lecture.

Identifying How Your Instructors Lecture 3-20

Write the name of each of your instructors. Use what you have learned to identify and write each instructor's lecture style(s).

Instructor	*Lecture Style*

ANSWER KEY

3-1 Responses will vary.
3-2 Number of statements checked will vary.
3-3 1. 92. 2. 436. 3 through 6. Responses will vary.
3-4 Responses will vary.
3-5 1. CIA. 2. NASA. 3. EST. 4. NATO. 5. eta. 6 through 10. Abbreviations will vary.
3-6 Responses will vary.
3-7 No response required.
3-8 1. Why people are placed in prison

2. A. Subtopic: retribution. Detail: repay debt to society.

   B. Subtopic: deterrence. Detail: less likely to commit another crime. Subdetail: the sentence should be long.

   C. Subtopic: rehabilitation. Detail: change criminals to conforming members of society. Detail: develop skills needed to succeed outside of prison. Subdetail: do not have to resort to crime.

   D. Subtopic: incapacitation. Detail: isolate criminals. Subdetail: keep them away from possible victims.

3. first, another, next, finally

3-9 1.

2. Responses will vary.

3-10 1. what, why

2. Commuter marriage

3. A. Question: What is a commuter marriage? Answer: Marriage in which the husband and wife work in different geographical locations. Supporting detail: Live together on weekends.

   B. Question: What are these marriages like? Answer: Lonely, hectic, hard to raise a family. Supporting details: Each partner lives alone. Family business must be done on the weekend. One partner has more responsibility for raising children.

   C. Question: Why will there be more commuter marriages? Answer: Women are pursuing careers in places other than where their husbands work. Supporting details: None in passage.

3-11 1.

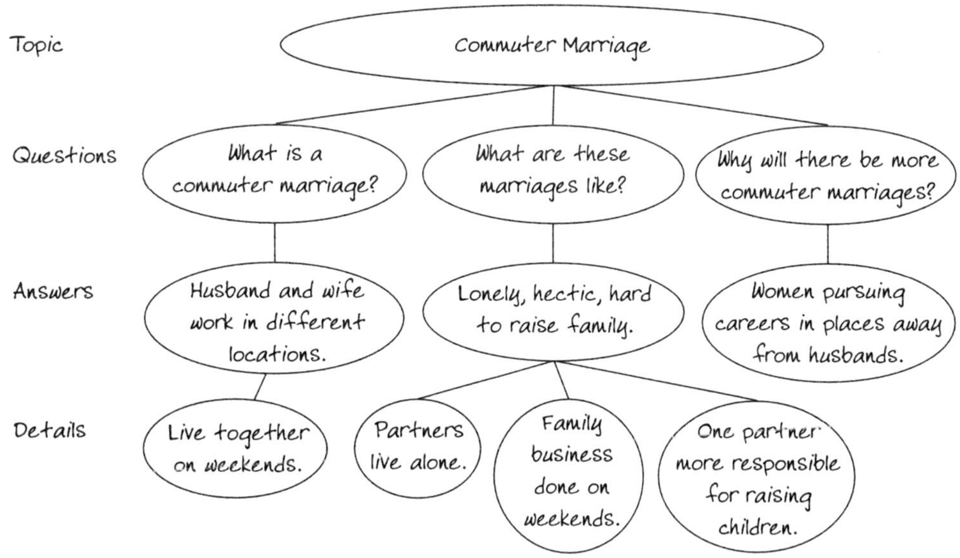

2. Responses will vary.

3-12 1. alike, distinct.

2. telephone and in-person poles.
3. used to obtain information, sample must represent the population, tone of voice can affect results, used by politicians.
4. Telephone polls: by telephone, inexpensive, use computer. In-person polls: face to face, how pollsters look can affect results.

3-13 1.

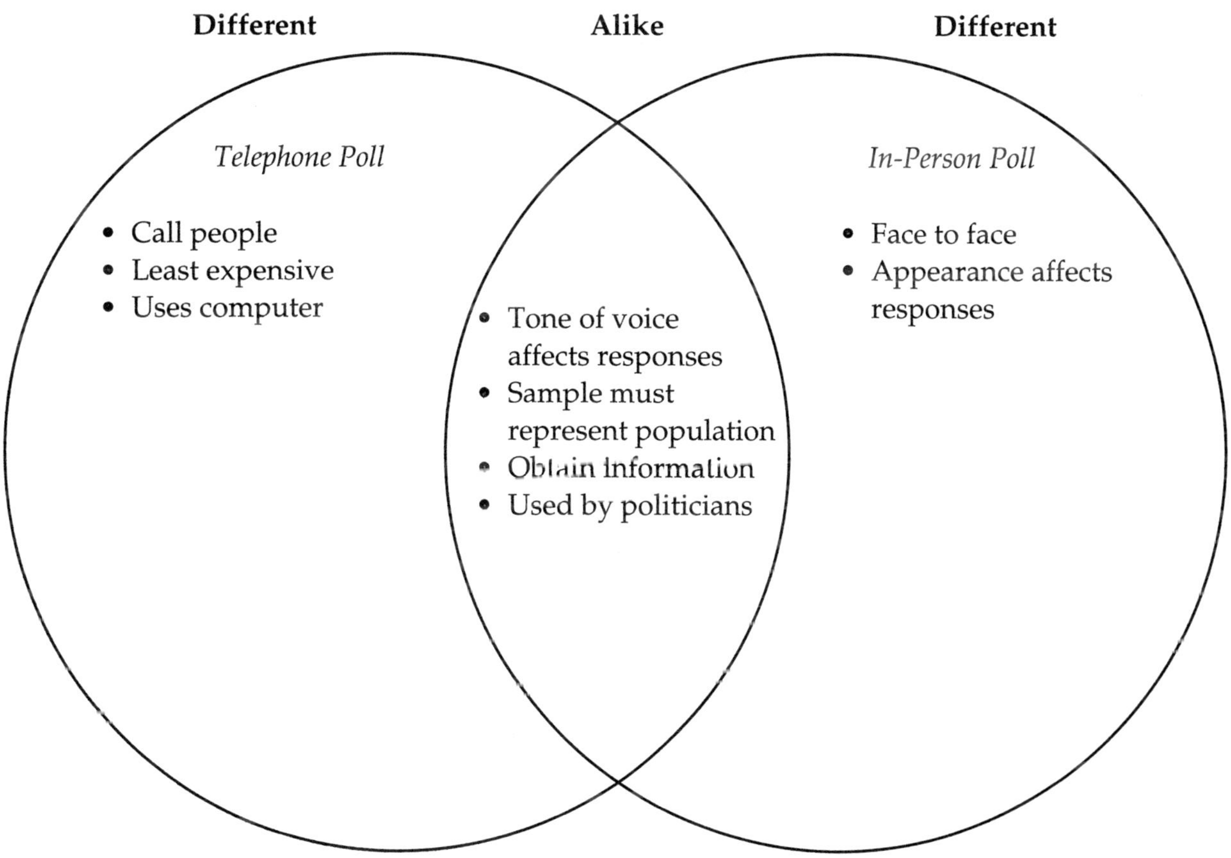

2. Responses will vary.

3-14 1. First, second, followed, next, finally
2. Declaration of Independence
3. 1620, Mayflower Compact
   Minimal rules for colonists
   1764, Sugar Act
   Taxes on products coming into colonies
   1765, Stamp Act
   Stamps needed for all documents
   1767, Townshend Acts
   Duties on all imports
   1774, First Continental Congress
   Declaration of Rights and Resolve
   1776, Second Continental Congress
   Declaration of Independence

3-15 1.

Topic	Declaration of Independence
First Event	1620, Mayflower Compact Minimal rules for colonists
	↓
Intervening Events	1764, Sugar Act Taxes on products coming into colonies 1765, Stamp Act Stamps needed for all documents 1767, Townshend Acts Duties on all imports 1774, First Continental Congress Declaration of Rights and Resolve
	↓
Final Event	1776, Second Continental Congress Declaration of Independence

3-16 1. because
2. Cause: high incidence of death and injury from front- end impact in automobile accident.
3. Effects and details:
   a. Effect: driver side air bags, (detail) passenger side airbags.
   b. Effect: remounted engines.
   c. Effect: stronger frames, (detail) extra metal supports in door frames.
   d. Effect: consumer education, (details) for adults; different for teenagers.

3-17 1.

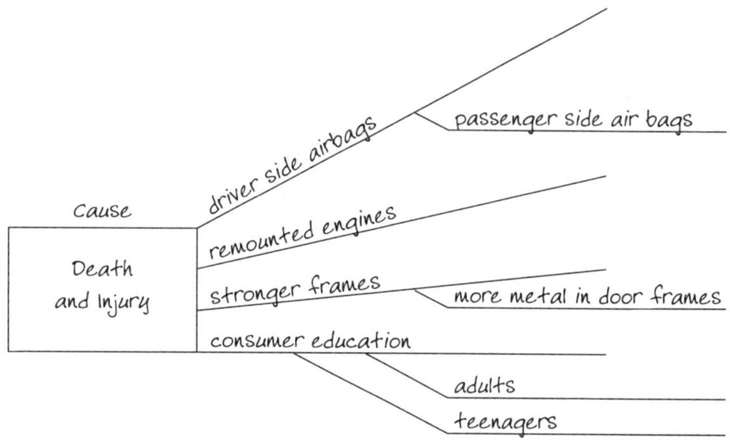

2. Responses will vary.

3-18 1. problem, solve
2. Problem: Coronary heart disease is a problem around the world.
3. Solutions and details:
   a. Solution: Eat less meat. Detail: Lowers fat and cholesterol.
   b. Solution: Stop using tobacco products. Detail: Smoking constricts blood vessels and raises blood pressure.
   c. Solution: More activity.
   d. Solution: Ideal body weight.

3-19 1.

Problem	Coronary heart disease
	↓
Why?	Killing many people
	↓
Attempted Solutions and Details	Eat less meat Less fat and cholesterol Stop using tobacco products Smoking constricts blood vessels and raises blood pressure More activity Be at ideal body weight
	↓
Solution or Status	Until recommendations are followed coronary heart disease will remain a problem

2. Responses will vary.

3-20 Responses will vary.

CHAPTER FOUR

Using Information Literacy Skills to Do Research

OBJECTIVES

1. **Teach students how to use the library to identify, evaluate, and select information in print and electronic formats for their class assignments, papers, and projects.**
2. **Teach students how to use the Internet to research information for their class assignments, papers, and projects.**

REPRODUCIBLE ACTIVITIES

4-1 Information Literacy and Research
4-2 A Strategy for Using Information Literacy Skills
4-3 The Library and the Internet
4-4 Learning about Tools to Find Information
4-5 Learning about Keywords
4-6 Learning about Boolean Connectors
4-7 Using Keywords and Boolean Connectors to Research Your Topic
4-8 Using Your Online Catalog
4-9 Using Abstracts and Indexes
4-10 Learning about the World Wide Web
4-11 Using the World Wide Web
4-12 Books and Other Materials Found in the Library
4-13 Using Books and Other Materials Found in the Library
4-14 Learning about Reference Sources
4-15 Using Reference Sources
4-16 Learning about Popular Magazines and Scholarly Journals
4-17 Using Popular Magazines and Scholarly Journals
4-18 Learning about Government Documents

4-19 Using Government Documents
4-20 Evaluating and Selecting Information from Library Resources
4-21 Finding Materials in the Library
4-22 Evaluating Information Found on the World Wide Web
Answer Key

USING REPRODUCIBLE ACTIVITIES

Here is a plan for using the chapter reproducible activities. Activities may be completed by students either independently or in class.

1. Use 4-1 and 4-2 to introduce students to information literacy and research, and to teach them a strategy for using information literacy skills.
2. Use 4-3 to teach students about the information found in a library and information found on the Internet.
3. Use 4-4 through 4-11 to teach students about the major tools used to identify and locate information, both in the library and on the Internet.
4. Use 4-12 through 4-19 to teach students about the various kinds of materials and formats of materials they can get in a library.
5. Use 4-20 through 4-22 to teach students how to find, evaluate, and select information that is believable and relevant for a topic.

Information Literacy and Research **4-1**

Information literacy is the ability to identify, select, and evaluate information in all formats in order to use it effectively. Information literacy is one of the three literacies required to function successfully in society today. It extends beyond the other two literacies: basic literacy and computer literacy.

Information literacy skills are necessary to conduct research. **Research** is the process of inquiry and investigation in which you examine issues, probe topics, and ask questions. You will be doing research in your classes when you write papers, complete projects, and do class presentations.

1. Define *research.*

2. Write a definition of *information literacy.*

3. List your assigned papers, projects, and class presentations for this semester that will require you to do research and use information literacy skills.

Course	***Assignment***	***Date Due***

A Strategy for Using Information Literacy Skills

4-2

Two places to **GO** for information are the library and the Internet. You must **USE** certain tools to access information in the library and **USE** other tools to access information on the Internet. From the library you **GET** books, articles, and other materials. From the Internet you **GET** information available on web pages. After you identify the information you need, you must **DO** two things with it: (1) evaluate the sources of the information and (2) select the most appropriate sources for your purposes. The following flowchart shows a strategy for using information literacy skills.

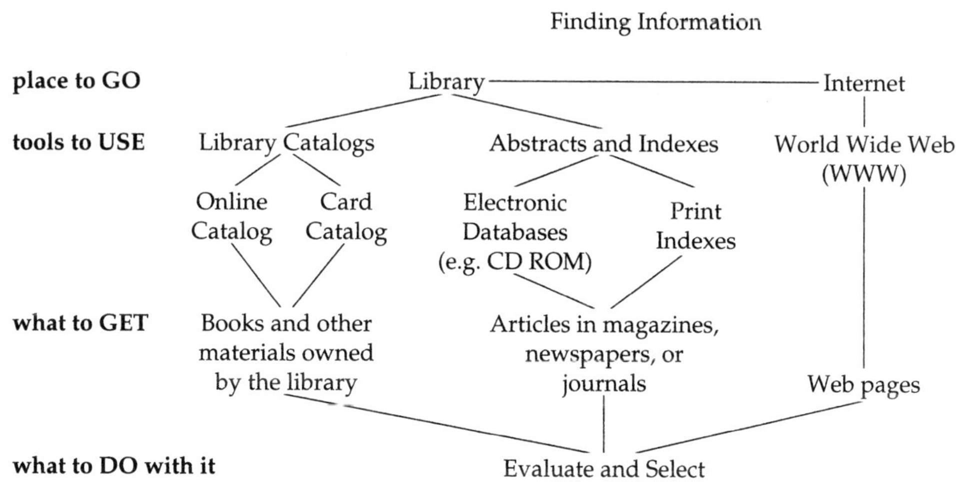

1. Where are two places to **GO** to locate information?

2. What tools do you **USE** in the library?

   On the Internet?

3. What can you **GET** in the library?

   On the Internet?

4. What two things must you **DO** with information?

The Library and the Internet

4-3

Places to GO

The library and the Internet are places you can **GO** to find information. With the availability of the Internet, you may wonder why you still have to use the library. Although more and more information is being made available on the Internet each day, only a portion of the world's information is currently available on the Internet. Therefore, the library remains an essential source of information for your research.

The Library

The library is the first place you should **GO** to find information. Your library has tools to **USE** to identify materials found there. Your library also has tools to use to identify information in sources not owned by your library. Most of the tools you use in libraries are in electronic format, although your library may still have some important tools in print format. In the library you can **GET** books, magazines, journals, and other materials that contain information. Much of the information available in libraries is in print format, although information such as newspaper and journal articles are increasingly being made available in electronic format.

The **Internet** is another place you can **GO** to find information. The Internet is a worldwide network of large computers and the cables that connect them. Information is available on computers connected to this network. The Internet allows you to use a personal computer to connect to and use information on this network. Anyone with access to the Internet can publish information on it. The World Wide Web (WWW) is the most important tool to **USE** to find information on the Internet. On the WWW you **GET** web pages that will lead you to a variety of information. However, many books and magazine and journal articles are not yet available on the WWW.

1. Write a paragraph that tells how you would use the library to find information.

2. Write a similar paragraph for the Internet.

Learning about Tools to Find Information **4-4**

Tools to USE

There are three major tools to **USE** to identify and locate information:

1. Library Catalogs (online and card)
2. Abstracts and Indexes (electronic and print)
3. World Wide Web

Library Catalogs

All libraries have a catalog listing materials found in the library. The catalog describes each item and tells where it is located.

Most academic libraries have an **online catalog** in which the information is entered into a computer. Libraries usually name their online catalogs (e.g., LUIS, MELVYL, ORBIS)

Some academic libraries also have a **card catalog** in which the information is typed on 3 × 5 cards and arranged alphabetically in file drawers. In these cases, the card catalog usually lists the older materials owned by the library. Card catalogs may also be used for specific collections within the library (e.g., Government Documents, Special Collections).

Abstracts and Indexes

These are sources used to identify articles in periodicals and newspapers. They are found in two formats: **electronic databases** and **print abstracts and indexes**.

Electronic databases are available in many subject areas. Because this is a new technology, most databases include information only from 1960 to the present. Most databases include just a summary of the article, but some include the full text in addition to a summary.

Print abstracts and indexes are available in many subject areas. Usually they are found in bound volumes. Each volume covers a certain period of time. Some print abstracts and indexes date from the nineteenth century.

World Wide Web

The WWW is a popular way to explore the Internet. However, the WWW contains only a portion of all information available in libraries. Information on the WWW is organized on *web pages*. The first or top page in a set of web pages is called the *home page*. Anyone with access to the WWW can create a web page and publish information on the Internet.

Visit your library to learn about the major tools at *your* library. Gather any handouts that will help you learn more about these tools. Ask the librarian if there are other instructional materials available to help you learn about these tools in your library (e.g., video, web tutorial).

Now answer the questions about tools in *your* library.

Library Catalogs

1. Does your library have an online catalog?

   If the online catalog has a name, write it here.

2. Can you connect to the online catalog from your home or dormitory ?

   Did you obtain information explaining how to do this?

3. What interesting facts did you learn about your online catalog?

4. Does your library have one or more card catalogs?

5. If yes, what did you learn about the card catalogs in your library?

Abstracts and Indexes

6. Where are the print abstracts and indexes located in your library?

7. Did you find a list of databases owned by your library?

8. Write the name of one full text database available in your library.

9. Can you connect to the databases from your home or dormitory?

   Did you obtain information explaining how to do this?

World Wide Web

10. Can you access the Internet to use the World Wide Web on computers in your library?

11. Does your library have its own web pages?

Learning about Keywords

4-5

You need a keyword to do a computer search on a topic. A keyword is an important word about your topic. Because computers do exactly what you tell them to do, you will probably need more than one keyword to focus your search. If you ask the computer to search for the keyword **teenager**, it will find all the records with the keyword **teenager**. It will *not* find other forms of the keyword **teenager** such as **teen** or **teenagers**. It will *not* find synonyms, such as **adolescent** or **adolescence**, or related terms such as **puberty**. Therefore, you should use more than one form of a keyword, such as its singular and plural forms, as well as synonyms and related terms for the keyword.

On the chart, write three words that can be used as keywords for the following topic: *Using computers to manufacture cars.* Then write other forms for each keyword as well as synonyms or related terms.

	1	2	3
Keywords			
Other Forms of Keyword			
Synonyms and Related Terms			

Learning about Boolean Connectors **4-6**

Boolean connectors are used to search for information in online catalogs, in electronic databases, and on the World Wide Web. The three Boolean connectors are: **and**, **or**, and **not.** The diagrams below illustrate the logic applied when a Boolean connector is used.

Connector	*Use*	*Example*	*Diagram*
and	Focus or narrow a search	environment **and** laws	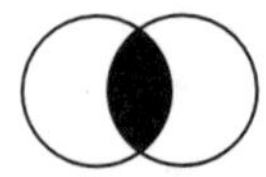
or	Expand or broaden a search	laws **or** legislation	
not	Exclude specific terms	environment **not** water	

As shown below, connectors may be used more than once in the same search. When you use more than one **or** along with **and** in the same search, you must put parentheses around the concepts with **or.** The parentheses tell the computer to combine the records with **or** before combining the records with **and**.

The example shows how Boolean connectors are used to combine terms related to the environment and law. This search will retrieve computer records with the keywords *environment* **or** *ecology* that also contain the keywords *law* **or** *legislation*. Records containing the keyword *water* will **not** be retrieved.

Connectors Used	*Example*
or, and, or, not	(environment **or** ecology) **and** (law **or** legislation) **not** water

Use Boolean connectors to combine the following terms in a search for information about funding for college sports other than football. Use parentheses where appropriate. The combination of keywords and Boolean connectors is called a **search statement**.

sports economics football universities funding colleges money athletics

Using Keywords and Boolean Connectors to Research Your Topic

4-7

1. Review the papers, projects, and class presentations you must do this semester. Select one that requires you to do research, and complete the following:

   I need to find information about the topic:

2. Underline words in your topic that you can use as keywords. Write these keywords on the chart. Write other forms of the keywords as well as synonyms and related terms.

	1	2	3
Keywords			
Other Forms of Keyword			
Synonyms and Related Terms			

3. Use Boolean connectors to combine your keywords. Use parentheses where needed. Write your search statement here.

Using Your Online Catalog

4-8

Tools to USE

Your library's online catalog contains information about each item owned by the library. Your library may have many computers with many different databases, but the online catalog is a good place to start. Your library also may have a card catalog containing information about older materials or special collections.

Every title in an online catalog has a computer **record.** The information on the record is arranged in **fields** (e.g., author, title, subject).

Review the papers, projects, and class presentations you must do this semester. Select one that requires you to do research. Use your library's catalog to look for information about the topic. For the topic, print one record for a *book* showing all the fields.

Answer these questions.

1. Under what subjects could you find this book?
2. What is its title?
3. Who wrote it?
4. In what year was it published?
5. Who is the publisher?
6. How many pages does the book contain?
7. Are there any illustrations?
8. What is the call number and location for this book?

Your online catalog may contain additional information about the materials that your library owns.

9. Check ✓ what you can find using your online catalog.

   ____ years of a specific newspaper owned by the library
   ____ whether a specific book is checked out
   ____ the latest issue of a specific magazine received by the library
   ____ whether a specific new book has been ordered
   ____ titles of materials found in branch libraries

Using Abstracts and Indexes

4-9

Tools to USE

Abstracts and indexes in electronic or print form are tools to **USE** to identify articles in popular magazines, newspapers, and scholarly journals. The three major categories of abstracts and indexes are **general, newspaper**, and **specialized**. There are many specific titles of abstracts and indexes for each of these categories.

General electronic databases and print abstracts and indexes cover a wide range of subjects and usually include popular magazines as well as selected scholarly journals. **Newspaper** electronic databases and print abstracts and indexes cover one or more newspapers. **Specialized** electronic databases and print abstracts and indexes cover specific disciplines such as psychology or education. Most electronic databases have a print version, which may cover more years than the database. Your library also may have some important print indexes that they do not have available in database form.

Go to your library to learn about the electronic databases and the print abstracts and indexes available. Ask your librarian if there are lists or handouts that describe these. Then complete the following:

1. (a) The title of a **general** database in my library is:

(b) The dates this database covers are:

(c) Write the title of the print version of this database or ✓ if there is no print version ____

(d) The dates covered by the print index are:

2. (a) The title of a **newspaper** database in my library is:

(b) The dates this database covers are:

(c) Write the title of the print version of this database or ✓ if there is no print version ____

(d) The dates covered by the print index are:

3. (a) The title of a **specialized** database for a specific discipline in my library is:

(b) The dates this database covers are:

(c) Write the title of the print version of this database or ✓ if there is no print version ____

(d) The dates covered by the print index are:

Learning about the World Wide Web

4-10

Tools to USE

The **World Wide Web (WWW)** allows you to travel around the world on the information superhighway. Information on the WWW is organized on **web pages**. The first or top page in a set of web pages is called the **home page**. One way to find a home page on the WWW is to use an address. The **Uniform Resource Locator (URL)** is the address of a web page. It often begins with: **http://**

You use the WWW to find information located on any of the servers connected to the Internet. The WWW allows you to jump from one Internet location to another by clicking on **linked** words. Linked words are connected to other pages of information. To use the WWW, you need a **web browser**. Some web browsers use **GUI (Graphical User Interface)** to present graphic images in addition to text. Some common web browsers are Netscape, Internet Explorer, and Mosaic. Other web browsers present text only. One of the most common text-only browsers is Lynx.

Answer these questions about access to the Internet at your school.

1. Where do you go to get a computer account? Do you have to pay for it?

2. List the locations of computer labs on campus where you can send and receive e-mail.

3. List the locations on campus where you can search the WWW using a GUI.

4. Does your computer account allow you to search the WWW from your home? Do you have to pay for it?

5. If you can search the World Wide Web from home with your computer account, does it use a GUI or is it text only?

6. What is the URL for your school's home page?

7. What other useful information did you find out about Internet access at your school?

Using the World Wide Web

4-11

Tools to USE

Following are examples of some web pages that might be useful for you when you do research. Next to each is its URL. Each of these web pages is organized by subject, with links to other web pages related to that subject.

The Argus Clearinghouse: A Selective Collection of Internet Guides
http://www.clearinghouse.net/
The WWW Virtual Library
http://www.w3.org/pub/DataSources/bySubject/Overview.html
EINet Galaxy http://www.einet.net/galaxy.html

Select one of these URLs and go to it on the WWW. "Surf" by clicking on links to other web pages, according to your interests. Select one of these other web pages that is of particular interest to you and write its URL here:

Answer these questions about the web page you selected.

1. On the computer screen, **hyperlinked words** or **hyperlinked phrases** are highlighted in different colors from the rest of the text. These hyperlinked words or phrases are linked to information anywhere on the WWW. Write at least two hyperlinked words or phrases found on the web page.

2. Some web pages have **navigation buttons** you can click on to jump to another page of information. What is the name of one navigation button on the home page?

3. The bottom of a web page often provides information about the individual who created or wrote the page. There may be a link to an **e-mail** address. This link allows visitors to send comments or otherwise communicate with the author. Does the web page you found have any information about the author or creator? Describe what you learned about the author or creator.

4. Is there an e-mail address on the home page? Write it here.

5. Is there a date indicating when the information was revised or updated? Write it here.

6. Why did you select this web page?

Books and Other Materials Found in the Library

4-12

What to GET

Read about the **resources** found in a library. Place a ✓ in front of each resource you have used in your library.

____ **Book:** Extensive coverage of a subject printed on paper that is bound together in a single volume.

____ **Reference Sources:** Materials to help you do research such as encyclopedias, almanacs, directories, and indexes. Usually these materials cannot be taken from the library.

____ **Newspaper:** A daily publication, usually daily, containing news and opinions about current events, feature stories, and advertising.

____ **Magazine:** A weekly or monthly publication, usually with glossy pictures and advertisements, which contains articles written by journalists on topics of general interest.

____ **Scholarly Journals:** A collection of articles written by experts in a specific field and published at regular intervals throughout the year, usually monthly or quarterly.

____ **Government Documents:** Materials published by local, state, federal, and international governments.

Read about the different **formats** in which these resources are found. Place a ✓ in front of each format you have used in your library.

____ **Print:** Sheets of paper, sometimes bound with a soft or hard cover.

____ **Microfiche:** Flat plastic cards, usually 4 x 6 inches, with reduced images, read or copied on reader/printers.

____ **Microfilm:** Small reels of film with reduced images that can be read or copied on reader/printers.

____ **Video cassette:** Cartridge containing magnetic tape with a filmed or televised image, usually including sound, and viewed using a television monitor and VCR.

____ **Audio cassette:** Small cartridge containing magnetic tape with recorded speech or sounds and listened to using a tape recorder.

____ **CD ROM** (Compact Disc Read Only Memory): A computer-based method of storing information as a database, requiring a computer and CD player for use.

____ **Multimedia:** Database that uses full text, video, sound, animation, and other features to provide information.

Using Books and Other Materials Found in the Library

4-13

What to GET

There are different kinds of **resources** found in the library: books, reference sources, newspapers, magazines, scholarly journals, and government documents. There are also different **formats** for these resources: print, microfiche, microfilm, video cassette, audio cassette, CD ROM, and multimedia.

1. Review the papers, projects, and class presentations you must do this semester. Select one that requires you to do research, and complete the following :

   I need to find information about the topic:

2. Use your library catalog and abstracts and indexes to identify three different **resources** that have information about this topic. Circle the three kinds of resources you identified.

   Scholarly Journal Magazine Newspaper Reference Source

   Book Government Documents

Write the title and the call number for each resource you circled. Also write the format for each resource.

Resource One

Resource Two

Resource Three

Learning about Reference Sources

4-14

What to GET

Reference sources are used to quickly find information on a topic. The most frequently used reference sources are encyclopedias, dictionaries, almanacs, atlases, biographical sources, and chronologies. Reference sources are available in the reference section of the library. Some reference sources are available in electronic format. Read about the different types of reference sources. Then answer the questions.

Types of Reference Sources

1. **Encyclopedia:** An encyclopedia contains articles on a variety of subjects written by experts. The articles are arranged in alphabetical order by topic.
   a. **General encyclopedias** include overview articles on a wide range of topics.
   b. **Single-volume encyclopedias** include short articles arranged in alphabetical order.
   c. **Foreign language encyclopedias** may be in a foreign language, or about a foreign country, or both.
   d. **Subject encyclopedias** are found for many specific subjects, such as medicine, psychology, art, music, business, science, or technology. The articles are longer, more complete, and more technical than those found in general encyclopedias.
2. **Dictionary:** A dictionary provides information about words.
   a. **Unabridged dictionaries** attempt to include all words currently in use in a language.
   b. **Abridged dictionaries** are shortened forms of unabridged dictionaries in which infrequently used words are omitted.
   c. **Etymological dictionaries** tell the history of words and explain how their meaning has changed over time.
   d. **Subject dictionaries** are found for many specific subjects, such as medicine, psychology, art, music, business, science, or technology. Subject dictionaries provide longer or more technical definitions of the terms and concepts for a discipline than do other types of dictionaries.
3. **Almanac:** An almanac is a single-volume reference book containing facts, data, tables, charts, lists, and other methods of organizing useful information. Most almanacs are updated yearly.
4. **Atlas:** An atlas is a collection of maps.
   a. **General world atlases** contain maps showing physical and political features of countries throughout the world. Most general world atlases include sections of maps on specific topics such as climate, population, or health.
   b. **Historical atlases** contain maps that portray an event or show how something developed or changed over a period of time. Historical atlases include information about topics such as changes in borders, military campaigns, exploration, or culture.
   c. **Subject atlases** contain maps related to a specific place or topic.

5. **Biographical sources:** These sources provide concise background information about the lives and accomplishments of famous people, living or dead. They are useful if you do not need or cannot find an entire book about a person.
6. **Chronology:** A chronology is a reference book that presents information organized by date. Chronologies may cover events over a long period of time, such as hundreds of years, or over as short a span of time as a single year. Some chronologies cover all subjects, whereas other chronologies cover specific subjects.

Answer the following questions about reference sources:

1. Where should you look to find the most complete definition of a technical word?
2. What is the difference between a general encyclopedia and a subject encyclopedia?
3. What is an almanac?
4. What kind of dictionary includes almost every word that people use today?
5. What kind of reference source arranges information by date?
6. What is a collection of maps bound together as a book called?
7. What is an abridged dictionary?
8. When would you use a biographical source?
9. When would you use an historical atlas?
10. Which type of encyclopedia includes articles on a wide variety of topics?
11. What are foreign language encyclopedias?
12. What is a subject atlas?

Using Reference Sources

4-15

What to GET

Identify and write the type of reference source you would use to find each of the following. As needed, refer to the descriptions of the most frequently used reference sources in 4-14.

1. The definition of Boolean logic.
2. Important events in art between 1850 and 1900.
3. Statistics about trade between the United States and Japan.
4. A map showing the boundaries of eastern European countries.
5. An overview of the life and works of Maya Angelou.
6. The definition of *transcendentalism.*
7. An overview article about the Monroe Doctrine.
8. A map that shows the major battles of World War II.
9. A short article about electronic databases.
10. The birth and death dates of Sir Winston Churchill.
11. A list of the five highest mountains in the world.
12. Definitions of the word *radical,* including how this word has been used throughout history.
13. A list of scientific discoveries during the nineteenth century.
14. An overview article about World War II written in German.
15. A long article that provides an overview about Romanticism in art.

Learning about Popular Magazines and Scholarly Journals

4-16

What to GET

Many of your research projects will require you to find information in articles. Articles in popular magazines are very different from articles in scholarly journals. To evaluate the information you find, you must understand how articles in popular magazines differ from articles in scholarly journals.

Popular magazines include **recreational**, **news,** and **opinion** magazines. **Recreational magazines** are written for general entertainment. Examples of recreational magazines are *People, Cosmopolitan,* and *Reader's Digest*. **News magazines** include general articles about current events and are written for the general public. Examples of news magazines are *Time, Newsweek,* and *U.S. News & World Report*. **Opinion magazines** offer commentary about current events from a specific point of view. They are written for an educated audience but are not focused on an audience in a specific discipline. Examples of opinion magazines are *The Nation, The New Republic,* and *National Review.*

Scholarly journals contain articles written by experts in a specific discipline. The articles present original research, reviews of research, or theoretical positions. Each discipline has its own scholarly journals. Examples of scholarly journals are: *JAMA: Journal of the American Medical Association, Journal of Educational Psychology,* and *Journal of the Academy of Marketing Science.*

Here are some characteristics of popular magazines and scholarly journals and the articles found within them. Write **P** in front of each characteristic of popular magazines and **S** in front of each characteristic of scholarly journals.

1. ____ are specialized for a specific discipline.
2. ____ articles do *not* include footnotes or a bibliography of sources.
3. ____ usually include glossy pages, many pictures, and advertisements.
4. ____ articles are written by scholars in the discipline.
5. ____ do not include original research, but may include stories about the research.
6. ____ use the terminology of a discipline.
7. ____ articles are written by journalists.
8. ____ have few glossy pictures and usually no advertisements.
9. ____ are often published by a professional organization.
10. ____ articles cite sources in footnotes or a bibliography.

Using Popular Magazines and Scholarly Journals

4-17

What to GET

Review the papers, projects, and class presentations you must do this semester. Select one that requires you to do research and complete the following:

I need to find information about the topic:

Complete the following activity for both a **popular magazine** and a **scholarly journal**.

Popular Magazine

1. Use an electronic database or a print abstract and index to identify an article about your topic found in a popular magazine. Write the complete citation.

2. Find the article in your library. Write its location and call number (if there is one).

3. Read the article and write three things you learned about your topic.

Scholarly Journal

4. Use an electronic database or a print abstract and index to identify an article about your topic found in a scholarly journal. Write the complete citation.

5. Find the article in your library. Write its location and call number (if there is one).

6. Read the article and write three things you learned about your topic.

Learning about Government Documents 4-18

What to GET

Government documents are materials published by a local, state, federal, or international government. Government documents can cover any subject area. They are published in all formats (e.g., microfiche, CD ROM) and include all types of resources (e.g., magazines, maps).

The Government Documents section of your library may have its own tools (e.g., card catalog, electronic database). Many government databases are on CD ROM. A large amount of government information is also available on the WWW. Your library may have one or more government document librarians to help you locate and use government documents.

Local documents are published by any agency or organization that is part of a city, municipality, or county government. Creators of local documents include the school board, the zoning commission, and the town clerk.

1. Write the name of another creator of local documents.

State documents are published by any agency or organization that is part of a state government. Creators of state documents include the legislature, the board of regents, and the bureau of prisons.

2. Write the name of another creator of state documents.

Federal documents are published by any agency or organization that is part of the United States government. Creators of federal information include the U.S. Congress, the National Park Service, the Armed Forces, the Department of Commerce, and the Environmental Protection Agency.

3. Write the name of another creator of federal documents:

International documents are published by any agency or organization that is part of the government of another country, or by any multinational organization formed by several governments. Creators of international documents include the United Nations (U.N.), the Organization of American States (OAS), and the North Atlantic Treaty Organization (NATO).

4. Write the name of another creator of international documents:

Using Government Documents

4-19

What to GET

Answer the following questions:

1. Does your library have a separate Government Documents section?
2. If yes, is there a desk or service point where you can get help?
3. If no, where are government documents located in your library?
4. Find one document for each of the following categories. For each document write the author, title, and call number as it appears in your card or online catalog.

Local Document

Author:

Title:

Call Number:

State Document

Author:

Title:

Call Number:

Federal Document

Author:

Title:

Call Number:

International Document

Author:

Title:

Call Number:

Evaluating and Selecting Information from Library Resources

What to DO with it

You must evaluate information to determine that it is believable before you select it for use. Your evaluation of the information should include both the author and the publication.

When evaluating the **author**, consider his or her credentials. Does the author have education and experience related to the topic? How many years has the author been working in the field? What research has the author conducted on this topic?

When evaluating the **publication**, consider how technical or how general it is. Is it a scholarly journal or a popular magazine? Is it biased or impartial? Is it an opinion, news, or recreational magazine?

Evaluate the following fictitious references about effective weight loss programs. Rate each reference on a believability scale of 1–3, where 1 = not believable, 2 = possibly believable, and 3 = believable. Write your rating next to each reference and explain the basis for your rating.

1. ____ An article in *People Magazine* on "Celebrity Diet Fads." The author has a B.A. in English and a master's degree in Journalism and is on the staff of writers for the magazine.
2. ____ An interview on *60 Minutes* with the surgeon general of the United States on "Weight Loss Clinics: The Fooling of America." The surgeon general is an M.D. who had 35 years' experience as a doctor and medical researcher.
3. ____ An article in the *Journal of Consulting and Clinical Psychology* called "The Effectiveness of Behavioral Weight Loss Programs: A Follow-Up Study." The author is a Ph.D in psychology and a tenured faculty member at a large research university.
4. ____ *The Lose-It Clinic Method: The Only Safe Way to Lose Weight* is a book written by the owner of the Lose-It Clinics, a national chain of weight-loss clinics under investigation by the Food and Drug Administration.
5. ____ Paper presented at the *Fourth International Conference on Obesity Management* about the National Hospital Mental Health Program in France, 1980–1990. The article is written by a psychiatrist on the staff of a major hospital in Paris.
6. ____ Newspaper article in the *New York Times*, "America's Most Popular Weight Loss Programs," written by the food editor.

After you evaluate the believability of a reference, you must evaluate its relevance to the topic. If a reference is not believable, do not use it. If a reference is possibly believable, obtain additional information from the publication to determine its believability. If a reference is believable, select it only if it is also relevant to the topic.

7. Circle the number of each reference above that you consider to be relevant as well as believable.

Finding Materials in the Library **4-21**

The Library of Congress, located in Washington, D.C., is the largest library in the United States. The system developed to organize this library is called the **Library of Congress (LC)** system. The LC system is used in most academic libraries. Books on similar subjects are grouped together under twenty primary classes, which are represented by letters of the alphabet. Here are the twenty primary classes of the LC system and the letter(s) that goes with each.

General Works	A	Music	M
Philosophy, Psychology, Religion	B	Fine Arts	N
Archaeology, Genealogy, Biography	C	Language and Literature	P
History: General and Old World	D	Sciences	Q
History: Americas	E–F	Medicine	R
Geography, Anthropology, Recreation	G	Agriculture	S
Social Sciences	H	Technology	T
Political Sciences	J	Military Science	U
Law	K	Naval Science	V
Education	L	Bibliography, Library Science	Z

Under what letter would you find books on the following topics:

1. ____ U.S. Civil War
2. ____ Spanish novels
3. ____ Buddhism
4. ____ Public school curriculum
5. ____ Sports
6. ____ Michelangelo
7. ____ Robots
8. ____ Cancer

When you locate an entry for a book in a card or online catalog, the book will be identified by a **call number**. A call number is a series of numbers or numbers and letters typed on a label on a book. The combination of letters and numbers is called **alphanumeric**. Look at these Library of Congress call numbers. They tell the subject of the book and the place where the book belongs on the shelf. They have been placed in correct alphanumerical order.

JK 560 .G78	JK 560 .R68	JK 560 .R7	JK 562 .R528	JK 562 .R53

9. Now use the numbers 1–5 to show the correct alphanumerical order of these call numbers.

HD 8066 .L38	HD 8066 .J38	HD 806 .L298	HD 8066 .L3224	HD 806.6 .L34
( )	( )	( )	( )	( )

Evaluating Information Found on the World Wide Web

4-22

Anyone can make information available on the World Wide Web. That's why you should question the believability of the information you find on the WWW. Here are four questions to answer and to help you evaluate the believability of the information.

Select a web page to complete this activity. Write down the URL for the web page you selected. Answer these questions for the web page located at your URL.

1. Is there anything that identifies the source of the information, such as the name of a company or organization? Sometimes that information is only on the top or home page. You may have to click on a navigation button for *home* to get to the home page. Write here anything you find about the company or organization that is providing the information.

2. Is the name of the author(s) anywhere on the page? Their e-mail address? Look at the top as well as the bottom. Write here the name and e-mail address of the author(s) or creator(s) of the information.

3. Is there any additional information that tells you about the author(s), such as professional position, education, or expertise? Write here anything you find out about the author(s) or creator(s) of the information.

4. Look at the bottom of the page. It might say "this page maintained by . . . " This may be the author(s) or a different person(s). Write here the name and e-mail address of the person(s) who maintains this page.

ANSWER KEY

4-1 1. Research is the process of inquiry and investigation in which you examine issues, probe topics, and ask questions. 2. Information literacy is the ability to identify, select, and evaluate information in all formats in order to use it effectively. 3. Responses will vary.

4-2 1. Library and the Internet. 2. Library catalogs: card and online; and abstracts and indexes: electronic and print; World Wide Web. 3. Books and other materials owned by the library; articles in magazines, newspapers, or journals; web pages. 4. Evaluate and select.

4-3 Responses will vary but should reflect the information presented in the activity.

4-4 Responses will vary.

4-5 Responses will vary, but an example is:

	1	2	3
Keywords	computers	manufacture	cars
Other Forms of Keyword	computer computing	manufacturing manufacturer manufacturers	car
Synonyms and Related Terms	automation technology robots	construct build produce	automobile automobiles vehicles

4-6 (sports **or** football **or** athletics) **and** (economics **or** funding **or** money) **and** (universities **or** colleges)

4-7 Responses will vary.

4-8 Responses will vary.

4-9 Responses will vary.

4-10 Responses will vary.

4-11 Responses will vary.

4-12 Responses will vary.

4-13 Responses will vary.

4-14 1. Subject dictionary. 2. General encyclopedias include overview articles on a wide range of topics, whereas subject encyclopedias are for specific subjects and include articles that are longer, more complete, and more technical than those found in general encyclopedias. 3. A single-volume reference book containing facts, data, tables, charts, lists, and other methods for organizing useful information. 4. Unabridged dictionary. 5. Chronology. 6. Atlas. 7. Shortened forms of unabridged dictionaries in which infrequently used words are omitted. 8. When you need concise background information about the lives and accomplishments of famous people, living or dead, and you do not need or cannot find an entire book about them. 9. To find a map that portrays an event or shows how something has developed or changed over a period of time. 10. General encyclopedia. 11. Encyclopedias in a foreign language or about a foreign country. 12. Contain maps related to a specific place or about a topic.

4-15 1. Subject dictionary. 2. Chronology. 3. Almanac. 4. Atlas. 5. Biographical source. 6. Unabridged or subject dictionary. 7. General encyclopedia. 8. Historical atlas. 9. Single-volume encyclopedia. 10. Biographical source. 11. Almanac. 12. Etymological dictionary. 13. Chronology. 14. Foreign language encyclopedia. 15. Subject encyclopedia.

4-16 1. S. 2. P. 3. P. 4. S. 5. P. 6. S. 7. P. 8. S. 9. S. 10. S.

4-17 Responses will vary.

4-18 Responses will vary.

4-19 Responses will vary.

4-20 Best answers are: 1. 2 = possibly believable. 2. 3 = believable. 3. 3 = believable. 4. 1 = not believable. 5. 3 = believable. 6. 2 = possibly believable. 7. 2, 3.

4-21 1. E–F. 2. P. 3. B. 4. L. 5. G. 6. N. 7. T. 8. R. 9. 5, 3, 1, 4, 2.

4-22 Responses will vary.

CHAPTER FIVE

Writing a Research Paper

OBJECTIVES

1. Teach students how to choose appropriate topics for a research paper.
2. Teach students how to document sources used in writing a research paper.
3. Teach students how to write a research paper.

REPRODUCIBLE ACTIVITIES

USING REPRODUCIBLE ACTIVITIES

Here is a plan for using the chapter reproducible activities. Activities may be completed by students either independently or in class.

1. Use 5-1 to introduce students to a strategy for writing a research paper.
2. Use 5-2 through 5-5 to teach students how to choose appropriate informative and persuasive topics and how to focus their research by establishing specific parameters.
3. Use 5-6 through 5-8 to teach students how to document their sources of information.
4. Use 5-9 through 5-14 to teach students how to write the different parts of a research paper.
5. Use 5-15 to teach students how to use a checklist to make certain that their paper is ready to hand in.

A Strategy for Writing a Research Paper **5-1**

A research paper is a paper that you write in which you cite information from a variety of sources. Research papers always include a bibliography of sources used or consulted. Follow these ten steps as you organize, write, and document your research paper:

Step 1. Choose a topic.
Step 2. Identify and select sources of information.
Step 3. Prepare bibliography cards to document the sources of information used.
Step 4. Prepare note cards to record information from each source used.
Step 5. Prepare an outline for the research paper.
Step 6. Write the research paper.
Step 7. Prepare footnotes to give credit to sources from which you quoted or took major ideas.
Step 8. Prepare a bibliography according to the style manual required by your instructor.
Step 9. Prepare a title page and table of contents.
Step 10. Proofread the research paper.

Review your course requirements to identify those courses for which you have to write a research paper. For each paper, write the topic, the name of the course, and the date the research paper is due.

Topic	***Course***	***Date Due***

Choosing a Topic

5-2

The first step in writing a research paper is to choose a topic. If the topic you choose is too broad, there will be too much information available and you may not be able to complete the research paper in the number of pages assigned. Choose a topic that has sufficient information but not so much that you will find it difficult to complete a paper about the topic.

Read each of the following topics. Each is too broad. Read to learn why each is too broad and what can be done to narrow it.

Topic: Health care in today's society.

This topic is too broad because there are many issues related to health care and society has many segments. To narrow this topic, you could select a specific issue, such as health care reform for a specific segment of society, such as the elderly. A better topic would be: *The implications of health care reform for the elderly in the United States.* This topic is sufficiently focused to complete a paper in the assigned number of pages.

Topic: Computers and education.

This topic is too broad because education needs to be narrowed down to a specific level of education (e.g., elementary school) and/or a subject area within education (e.g., science). A better topic would be: *Using computers to teach science in elementary schools.*

Each of the following topics is too broad. Narrow and rewrite each topic to make it appropriate for a research paper.

1. World hunger

2. The history of Chinese culture

3. U.S. foreign policy in Latin America

4. Review your topics from 5-1. Where necessary, rewrite your topic to make it appropriate.

Informative and Persuasive Topics **5-3**

When a research paper provides information without the writer's own point of view, it is an **informative** research paper. When the writer presents the information to support a point of view or to argue against an alternative point of view, it is a **persuasive** research paper. For example:

> *Movie themes of the 1990s* is an informative topic.
> *Movies should not be rated* is a persuasive topic.

Place **I** in front of topics that suggest an informative research paper, and **P** in front of topics that suggest a persuasive research paper:

1. _____ Homeless children in America

2. _____ Some athletes with AIDS should be banned from playing their sport

3. _____ The message of rap music

4. _____ Censorship of college newspapers

5. _____ Athletes and AIDS

6. _____ The need for increased funding for the homeless

7. _____ Drug testing in our public schools: Is it really necessary?

8. _____ Rap music causes teenage violence

9. _____ Drugs in our schools

10. _____ Using robots to build cars

Practice Writing Persuasive Topics 5-4

Some of your research papers will be assigned as persuasive papers. A persuasive paper is written to support or oppose a point of view. In the following example, a point of view was used to change an informative topic into a persuasive topic.

Informative: Competition between Japanese and American automobile manufacturers
Persuasive: Japanese cars are better than American cars.

Rewrite each topic to make it persuasive.

1. Advertising on television

2. Dress codes in public schools

3. Political parties in the United States

4. The increasing world population

5. Day care centers for children of working mothers

6. The U.S. government's foreign policy on Iraq

7. Forms of capital punishment in the United States

8. Salaries for professional athletes

Focusing Your Research **5-5**

Select one of your topics from 5-1 and write it here:

Before you begin to write your paper and search for information, you must be specific about the kind of paper you will write and the information you will need. Answering these questions will help you focus your research. Use a check (✓) to show your answers.

1. Will this be a paper only, or is there an oral presentation as well?

   Written paper ____

   Written paper and oral presentation/speech ____

2. Which visual aids do you need to include?

   Pictures ____ Photographs ____ Graphs ____ Charts ____ Maps ____

   Other visual aids? Write them here.

3. What should be the length of your paper?

   1 to 5 pages ____ 6 to 10 pages ____ More than 10 pages ____

4. Is your paper
   informative? ____ persuasive ____?

5. Do you need any historical information? Yes ____ No ____

6. Do you need information from within the last year? Yes ____ No ____

7. Are there terms or concepts associated with this topic that you do not understand?

   Yes ____ No ____ List them.

8. Are there questions that must be answered with numbers or statistics?

   Yes ____ No ____ Write them here.

Locating Sources of Information **5-6**

Write the topic you selected in 5-5:

Find information on your topic in the library or on the Internet. Locate as many sources as needed to complete your paper. Use at least one source from each of the following categories to obtain information to write your paper. Write the title for one source from each category. Place a ✓ in front of the title for each source found in an electronic format. In 5-7 you will prepare bibliography cards for these sources.

Encyclopedia

____ Title:

Other Reference Book

____ Title:

Popular Magazine

____ Title:

Newspaper

____ Title:

Scholarly Journal

____ Title

Book

____ Title:

Government Document

____ Title:

Audio/Visual

____ Title:

World Wide Web

Title of web page:

Documenting Your Sources 5-7

In a research paper you must give credit to sources from which you took ideas. Using another person's words, thoughts, or ideas without giving credit is plagiarism. Credit is given by documenting the source of the information in the bibliography you will prepare for your paper.

Bibliography cards are used to keep a record of the sources from which you obtained information for your paper. Examine the sample bibliography cards prepared for a wide variety of sources. Then prepare bibliography cards to document the sources you found in 5-6.

Book

Perkins, David N. Software Goes to School: Teaching for Understanding with New Technologies. New York: Oxford University Press, 1995.

Magazine Article

Smith, Gina. "Schools of the Future? (Integration of Computers in the Classroom)." Popular Science July 1996:26.

Government Document

United States. Department of Education. A Perspective on Reform in Mathematics and Science Education. Washington: GPO, 1996.

Audio/Visual

Multimedia Technology, Program 6, Environments for Learning. Writers Jeff Nielson and Rich Reeder. Videocassette. Minnesota Satellite and Technology, 1995.

World Wide Web

Author:	Grant, Peter
Title:	For Science Teachers and Students
Date of Information:	15 Dec. 1996.
Site:	New South Wales Technical and Further Education Commission.
URL:	http://www/webcom.com/~pjgrant
Online Service:	World Wide Web, Netscape.
Date Accessed:	December 29, 1996

Reference Book

Clements, Douglas H. and Nastasi, Bonnie K. "Electronic Media and Early Childhood Education." Handbook of Research on the Education of Young Children. Ed. Bernard Spodek, New York: Macmillan Publishing Co., 1995. 258-259.

Journal Article

Allen, Denise. "Teaching with Technology: Bytes of Math and Science." Teaching PreK-8 26.4 (1996):16-18.

Newspaper Article

MacFarquhar, Neil. "The Internet Goes to School: Bellweather or Bust? Educators Debate Value of Surfing." New York Times 7 Mar. 1996, nat'l ed.: Bl.

Electronic Database

Author:	Spaid, Elizabeth Levitan.
Title of Article:	"More U.S. School Districts Start to Wire Classrooms for the Information Age."
Title of Publication:	Christian Science Monitor
Date of Article: Pages:	2 Mar. 1993:1+
Title of Database:	SIRS CD ROM.
Publication Medium:	CD ROM.
Vendor Location and Name:	Boca Raton: SIRS.
Date of CD ROM:	1996.

Preparing Note Cards **5-8**

Look at the sample bibliography card and corresponding note cards as you read to learn about notecards.

Bibliography Card

3

Barlow, Libby. <u>Internet in the Classroom: A Primer for Education</u>. Guildford, CT: Talcott Press, 1997.

NoteCards

(3-1)

-Classroom instruction changing
-active learning—cooperative learning
-imperative to develop "critical thinking in the information age."

(3-2)

Government funding for schools
-state and federal support for
inf
-Pr
-Pr
sup

(3-3)

Staff development for teachers
-teachers need time off to learn
-workshops, continuing education necessary
-partner with higher education to share development resources
-preparing the next generation of teachers

Note cards are used to record notes from each source you used when writing a research paper. Before you prepare note cards, you must arrange your bibliography cards in alphabetical order by the first word on the card. When alphabetizing, ignore initial articles such as *A*, *An*, or *The*. Then number the bibliography cards starting with "1" for the first card. The number should be written in the upper right-hand corner of the bibliography card (see sample bibliography card). Once you have alphabetized and numbered the bibliography cards, you are ready to prepare note cards.

Number your note cards using two numbers separated by a dash (see sample note cards). On a note card numbered 2-1, 2 shows that the notes are for the source listed on bibliography card 2, and -1 shows this is the first card used to record notes from this source. If you need more than one note card to record notes from this source, the second card would be numbered 2-2, the third card 2-3, and so on. Write the number of the note card in the upper right-hand corner of the card. Circle the number to keep it separate from any other numbers you might write when taking notes.

Write notes in your own words whenever possible. Use abbreviations and symbols except for quotes, which must be cited exactly as they appear in the source. Place quotation marks around all quotes. Write the page number on which each quote appears. Look at the following bibliography card and a note card that goes with it. Answer the questions that follow.

Sample Bibliography Card

```
Brown, Bill. "Siteseeing on the Net: Science Museums go online."   4
K-12 Internet News, Nov. 1996: 11-14.
```

Sample Note Card

```
"Major science museums provide virtual tours through their web   (4-2)
pages" p 11
Schools need to be wired to access the WWW
Many sci museums have interactive instructional materials
Multimedia web sites req upgraded computers in classrooms for
graphics, sound, & video, etc.
```

1. Describe how you should you place bibliography cards in alphabetical order?

2. Where on a bibliography card should you write its number?

3. Why is the number 4-2 circled on the note card?

4. What does the 4 tell you?

5. What does the -2 tell you?

6. What does the number 4-3 on a note card mean?

7. Can you have more than one note card for a bibliography card?

8. When should you use quotation marks on a note card?

Prepare note cards for the bibliography cards you prepared in 5-7.

Writing an Outline for a Research Paper **5-9**

Examine the sample outline. Use the notes from your note cards to prepare a similar outline for your research paper. Organize your information according to topics, subtopics, details, and subdetails. Then write the title of your paper near the top of a blank piece of paper. As shown in the sample outline below, use numerals and letters to create your outline. Use Roman numerals for topics, capital letters for subtopics, Arabic numerals for details, and lower-case letters for subdetails. You may write the topics, subtopics, details, and subdetails as sentences, phrases, or single words. The number of subtopics, details, and subdetails can vary for each topic.

Using Computers to Teach Science in Elementary School

Topic	I. Types of computer resources available for science education
Subtopic	A. Multimedia
Detail	1. Product reviews
Subtopic	B. Software
Detail	1. Product reviews
Subdetail	a. Trade magazines
Subdetail	b. Education publications
Subtopic	C. Internet
Detail	1. WWW sites for teachers
Detail	2. WWW sites for students
Detail	3. Using e-mail as a teaching tool
Topic	II. Political and financial aspects
Subtopic	A. Getting schools wired and computers into the classrooms
Detail	1. Federal funds
Detail	2. Partnerships with industry
Detail	3. Grant sources
Subtopic	B. Censorship issues
Detail	1. Parental role
Topic	III. Training teachers
Subtopic	A. Defining competencies
Subtopic	B. Sharing responsibility
Detail	1. Role of school board, profession, and individuals
Subtopic	C. Creating opportunities for continuing education

Writing the Research Paper **5-10**

Begin by writing a rough draft of your research paper. Leave at least one-inch margins on all sides, and double space the draft to leave room for revising. Number each page in the top right-hand corner.

Type the title of your paper at the top of the page. Then write an introduction that tells the reader what your paper is about. Use your outline and note cards to write the body of the paper. As you write, insert headings and visual aids to help the reader understand your topic. If you are writing an informative paper, end with a conclusion that tells the reader what you have learned about the topic. For a persuasive paper, end by summarizing your point of view.

Use the Revising Checklist to learn what changes you may need to make in your rough draft. Place a ✓ next to each question for which you can answer "yes." Revise your draft until you can check Yes to all the questions.

Revising Checklist

____ **1.** Does the introduction clearly introduce the topic?

____ **2.** Did I include headings to help the reader understand the topic?

____ **3.** Does the body of the paper contain all the facts needed?

____ **4.** Does each paragraph contain a main idea?

____ **5.** Does each paragraph add something to the paper?

____ **6.** Did I choose the best words to explain my ideas?

____ **7.** Did I include a conclusion for an informative paper or a summary for a persuasive paper?

____ **8.** Did I spell all words correctly?

____ **9.** Did I capitalize words as needed?

____ **10.** Do all sentences have subject-verb agreement?

____ **11.** Are tenses consistent?

____ **12.** Are all sentences complete?

____ **13.** Did I use quotation marks to identify all quotations?

____ **14.** Have I reread the paper several times to find ways to improve it?

____ **15.** Did I number the pages correctly?

Preparing Footnotes 5-11

Footnotes are used to document each source of information you use. They identify who wrote the information and the page or pages where it is found. Footnote reference numbers are written immediately after the information in the text for which credit is being given. The numbers are small and slightly raised above the line. Most commonly, footnotes are placed at the bottom of the page of the research paper that contains the information or quotation cited, with a horizontal line separating the text from the footnotes.

Examine the sample text and its corresponding footnotes.

> Educators believe that college students spend too much time playing computer games that have little to do with learning.[1] Mary Lehrer, President of the American Council of Research on Undergraduate Education, wrote in the Council's newsletter that ". . . computer games are addictive and encourage sexist and aggressive behaviors."[2] Karl Ages, President of the International Society of Computer Games, argues that "Electronic games contribute to the acquisition of basic computer skills, and are relaxing and fun."[3]
>
> ---
>
> 1. Thomas Proff, America's College Students (Newark: Orbis Press, 1996) 17.
> 2. Mary Lehrer, "Motivating Students," Newsletter of the American Council of Research on Undergraduate Education, 28 (December 1996): 12.
> 3. Karl Ages, "Computer Games for the Future," CD Mag, Jan. 1997:40.

Sometimes your instructor will prefer to have all the footnotes on one page at the end of the paper. When footnotes are listed at the end of a paper, the same format is used for writing the footnotes. The footnotes are numbered in the order the information is presented in the paper. Ask your professor which way you should show the footnotes in your research paper.

1. Why do you use footnotes in a research paper?

2. In what two places can footnotes be placed?

3. How do you know in which place footnotes should appear in your paper?

Read your research paper and add footnotes to document sources used.

Preparing a Bibliography

5-12

At the end of your research paper you must provide a list of all the sources you used or consulted to write your paper. This list of sources is called the **bibliography**. To prepare a bibliography, arrange your bibliography cards in alphabetical order by the first word on each card. When alphabetizing, ignore initial articles such as *A*, *An*, or *The*. For example, in the sample bibliography below, the entry for *A Perspective on Reform in Mathematics and Science Education* is alphabetized using the word *Perspective*.

After you arrange your bibliography cards in correct alphabetical order, type the word *Bibliography* at the top of a sheet of paper. Now type the information as it appears on each bibliography card. Indent the second and following lines as shown in the following bibliography.

Bibliography

Allen, Denise. "Teaching with Technology: Bytes of Math and Science." Teaching PreK–8 26.4 (1996) : 16–18.

Clements, Douglas H. and Nastasi, Bonnie K. "Electronic Media and Early Childhood Education." Handbook of Research on the Education of Young Children. Ed. Bernard Spodek, New York: Macmillan, 1995. 258–259.

Grant, Peter. For Science Teachers and Students. 15 Dec. 1996. New South Wales Technical and Further Education Commission. http://www/webcom.com/~pjgrant World Wide Web, Netscape. December 29, 1996.

MacFarquhar, Neil. "The Internet Goes to School: Bellweather or Bust? Educators Debate Value of Surfing." New York Times 7 Mar. 1996, national edition: B1.

Multimedia Technology. Program 6, Environments for Learning. Writers Jeff Nielson and Rich Reeder. Videocassette. Minnesota Satellite and Technology, 1995.

Perkins, David N. Software Goes to School: Teaching for Understanding with New Technologies. New York: Oxford University Press, 1995.

Smith, Gina. "Schools of the Future? (Integration of Computers in the Classroom)." Popular Science July 1996: 26.

Spaid, Elizabeth Levitan. "More U.S. School Districts Start to Wire Classrooms for the Information Age." Christian Science Monitor 2 Mar. 1993:1+. SIRS CD ROM. CD ROM. Boca Raton: SIRS, 1996.

United States Department of Education. A Perspective on Reform in Mathematics and Science Education. Washington: GPO, 1996.

Prepare the bibliography for your research paper. You may use the format provided in this activity, or one that your instructor requires.

Preparing a Title Page 5-13

The **title page** is the first page of a research paper. It should include the title of the research paper, the name of the writer, the course number and section, semester, instructor, and date the paper is due.

To prepare the title page, start by typing the title on a sheet of paper. Be sure to center the title and use all caps or boldface type to highlight it. Three lines below the title, center and type the word *by*. Three lines below the word *by*, center and type your name. Two lines below your name, center and type the date that the paper is due. Four lines from the bottom margin, center and type *For:* followed by your instructor's name. On the next line, center and type the course number and section. On the next line, center and type the semester.

Look at the sample Title Page.

USING COMPUTERS TO TEACH SCIENCE IN ELEMENTARY SCHOOL

by

Pasqualina Browne

August 8, 1997

For: Professor Mary Lehrer
ED 3892, Section 4
Summer B, 1997

Prepare the title page for your research paper. You may use the format provided in this example, or one that your instructor requires.

Preparing a Table of Contents **5-14**

The **table of contents** is the second page of the research paper. It lists the main topics and important subtopics and the page on which each is introduced. To prepare a table of contents, type "Table of Contents" at the top of a sheet of paper, with the first letter of the word "Table" and the first letter of the word "Contents" capitalized. Capitalize each major word in each entry. You may use dots to connect the entry to the page number, as shown in the example.

Table of Contents

Prepare the table of contents for your research paper. You may use the format provided in this example, or one that your instructor requires.

Final Checklist **5-15**

When you have finished writing your research paper, use the Final Checklist to make certain your paper is ready to be handed in. Place a ✓ next to each question for which you can answer "yes." If you have a ✓ next to all questions, your paper is ready to be handed in to your instructor. If not, revise your paper until you have a ✓ next to all questions. Then your paper is ready to be handed in.

Final Checklist

____ **1.** Do I have a title page?

____ **2.** Do I have a table of contents?

____ **3.** Are the pages numbered correctly?

____ **4.** Have I included all the footnotes?

____ **5.** Does the bibliography include all the sources I used?

____ **6.** Do I have a second copy for my files?

ANSWER KEY

5-1 Responses will vary.

5-2 1. Responses will vary, but should show more focused topic, such as "world" narrowed down to a specific country. 2. Responses will vary, but should show more focused topic, such as a particular period of history, or a specific aspect of Chinese culture. 3. Responses will vary, but should show more focused topic, such as a specific aspect of foreign policy for a specific country in Latin America. 4. Responses will vary.

5-3 1. I. 2. P. 3. I. 4. I. 5. I. 6. P. 7. P. 8. P. 9. I. 10. I.

5-4 Responses will vary, but new topics should show a point of view.

5-5 Responses will vary.

5-6 Responses will vary.

5-7 Bibliography cards will vary.

5-8 1. By the first word on the card, ignoring initial articles. 2. Upper right-hand corner. 3. To keep it separate from other numbers you might write while taking notes. 4. The number of the bibliography card from which the notes were taken. 5. The second card used to take notes from this source. 6. The third note card from bibliography card 4. 7. Yes. 8. For quotes.

5-9 Outlines will vary.

5-10 Responses will vary.

5-11 1. To document the sources of information used by identifying who wrote the information and where it appeared. 2. At the bottom of the page that contains the information or quotation cited, or at the end of the paper. 3. Your instructor will tell you.

5-12 Bibliographies will vary.

5-13 Title pages will vary.

5-14 Table of Contents will vary.

5-15 Responses will vary.

CHAPTER SIX

Preparing for and Taking Tests

OBJECTIVES

1. **Teach students a five-day strategy for preparing to take tests.**
2. **Teach students a strategy for improving their test scores.**
3. **Teach students strategies for taking essay and objective tests.**

REPRODUCIBLE ACTIVITIES

USING REPRODUCIBLE ACTIVITIES

Here is a plan for using the chapter reproducible activities. Activities may be completed by students either independently or in class.

1. Use 6-1 through 6-2 to teach students how to prepare for tests.
2. Use 6-3 to teach students a strategy for improving their test scores.
3. Use 6-4 through 6-11 to teach students a strategy for taking essay tests. For 6-7, students will need to know the graphic organizers taught in Chapters One and Three.
4. Use 6-12 through 6-18 to teach students how to take objective tests.

Preparing for a Test

Success on a test begins before you take a test. Read to learn about what you must do to prepare for a test. As you read a statement, think about how you would do what it suggests.

1. Ask your instructor what the test will cover. Ask what you need to study from your textbooks, handouts, and class notes. Also ask what will not be on the test, so that you will know exactly what to study.

2. Ask your instructor what types of items will be on the test—multiple choice? True–false? Matching? Completion? Essay? Instructors often use more than one type of item on a test. Knowing what type of items will be on a test can guide the way you will study.

3. Begin studying for your test early. Allow at least five days to study. You will need at least this much time to review and master the information that will be on the test.

Write a summary paragraph that tells how you will prepare for your next test.

Five-Day Test Preparation Plan **6-2**

Once you know what a test will cover and the types of test items to expect, begin following the five-day test preparation plan. If you follow this plan, each day you will find yourself more ready to take the test.

Day Five	Review what you need to study from your textbooks, handouts, and class notes. Highlight or underline the important information.
Day Four	Rewrite the information you highlighted or underlined in as few words as possible. Use these rewritten notes to review the information at least twice on this day.
Day Three	Use graphic organizers, acronyms, abbreviations, acronymic sentences, pegwords, keywords, and/or rhyme to help you remember the information in your rewritten notes. Review the information at least twice on this day.
Day Two	Use your rewritten notes to make a list of questions you think will be on the test. Write answers for these questions. Review the questions and answers several times on this day.
Day One	This is the day you take the test. Review the questions and answers you developed. Do this once before you go to class and again while you are in class waiting for the instructor to begin the test.

In your own words, describe what you should do on each day.

Day Five:

Day Four:

Day Three:

Day Two:

Day One:

Using the DETER Strategy to Improve Your Test Score

6-3

The **DETER** strategy consists of five procedures you should follow to improve your score on any test.

1. Read the test **Directions** carefully. Ask your instructor to explain anything you do not understand.

2. **Examine** the entire test to see how much there is to do. Do this immediately after you have read and made certain you understand the test directions.

3. Decide how much **Time** you should spend answering each item on the test. Consider how many items are on the test and how many points each is worth. Spend the most time on the items that count for the most points.

4. Begin by answering the **Easiest** items. Then answer as many of the remaining items as you can. If there is no penalty for answering incorrectly, try to answer all items.

5. **Review** your answers before handing in the test.

Write a statement explaining what each letter in **DETER** reminds you to do.

D

E

T

E

R

The QUOTE Strategy for Taking Essay Tests: Question Step

6-4

QUOTE is an acronym for a strategy you should follow when answering essay test items. The five steps of the strategy are:

Question
Underline
Organize
Time
Evaluate

Q **Question** is the first step you should apply in the **QUOTE** strategy. Begin by asking the **Q**uestion, "What is/are the direction word(s) in the test item?" Identify and bracket [] the direction word(s). For example:

Around the world women and their activities are held in less esteem than men and their activities. Further, in all societies women have been systematically discriminated against in social life. [Explain] how female minority status came about.

Here are three direction words and their definitions:

Discuss means to give reasons behind different points of view.
Describe means to present a detailed picture of something.
Explain means to give the reasons for something.

Bracket [] the direction word in each of the following essay items.

1. When a continuous reinforcement schedule is used as part of a behavioral program, every occurrence of a target behavior is reinforced. Describe a situation in which a teacher might wish to use a continuous reinforcement schedule.
2. Microsociology focuses on social interaction, whereas macrosociology focuses on social structure. Explain why both are necessary for an understanding of social life.
3. The Eighth Amendment of the Constitution prohibits "cruel and unusual punishment." However, the question of what is "cruel and unusual" has been controversial for the Supreme Court. Using your knowledge of constitutional law, discuss interpretations of "cruel and unusual" that have appeared in the Court's rulings over the past thirty years.

Write an essay item using the direction word **discuss**. Do the same for **describe** and **explain**. Choose your own topics for the items.

More Direction Words

Here are more direction words you will find in essay test items. Sometimes a different form of the direction word is used, such as *relationship* for *relate* or *summary* for *summarize.*

List means to present information in some order.
Trace means to state a series of things in logical order.
Relate means to show how two or more things are connected.
Diagram or **illustrate** means to create a visual representation in order to demonstrate, explain, or clarify something.
Compare means to tell how two or more things are alike as well as different.
Contrast means to tell only how two or more things are different.
Criticize means to make positive and negative comments about something.
Evaluate means to judge something using an established set of criteria.
Summarize means to state the major points about something.

For each of the following essay items, bracket [] the direction word and explain what the direction word is telling you to do.

1. What is the relationship between cognitive effort and long-term memory?

2. Use the criteria in your textbook to evaluate this painting by Van Gogh.

3. Construct a diagram that represents the reinforcement–affect model of how emotions determine attraction.

4. Trace the important events leading to the resignation of Richard Nixon as president of the United States.

5. Contrast the political platforms of the Democratic and Republican parties.

6. Develop a list of the factors that contribute to overweight.

7. Read the article by Jonathan While. Then write a summary of his position on social welfare reform in the United States.

8. Write a critique of the recent performance of *King Lear* staged by our Department of Theater and Dance.

9. In this class, you have learned about the platforms of the Democratic and Republican parties. Write a statement that compares their platforms.

Write an essay item using the direction word **list**. Do the same for the other direction words in this activity.

QUOTE: Underline Step

U **Underline** is the second step in the **QUOTE** strategy. After you have bracketed [] the direction word, underline the focus words that help you focus on the ideas to be developed in the answer. Study the following example:

Blood glucose levels are regulated by the pancreas. Whenever blood sugar levels are too high, the pancreas releases a hormone called <u>insulin</u>. [Explain] the <u>mechanism</u> by which insulin <u>lowers</u> the level of <u>blood sugar</u> in the body.

For each of the following essay items, [] the direction word and underline the focus words.

1. The Constitution of the United States is a set of written laws and principles. Explain what the Founding Fathers set out to accomplish when they wrote this document.

2. Exercise should be an important part of everyone's life. Describe the ways in which exercise can help one lead a longer, healthier, and more fulfilling life.

3. Controversy still exists regarding whether the United States was right to engage in the Vietnam War. Considering different views, trace the events that led to this war.

4. Construct a diagram that shows the incremental effects of group size on relationships.

5. A cognitive view of persuasion has largely replaced the traditional view of persuasion. Compare these two views.

QUOTE: Organize/Write Step

6-7

O **Organize/Write** is the third step in the **QUOTE** strategy. For this step do the following:

1. *List the facts you know.* On scrap paper list all the facts you know that are related to the focus words you underline in an essay test item.
2. *Organize your facts.* Create a graphic organizer to organize your facts. Use one of the graphic organizers you learned about in Chapters One and Three (topic–list, question–answer, compare–contrast, series of events, cause–effect, problem–solution).
3. *Write your answer using your graphic organizer as a guide.*
   - Here is what to do when writing a one-paragraph answer to an essay test item: Begin with a sentence that contains your main point. Follow this with sentences that support your point. End your answer with a sentence that states your conclusion.
   - Here is what to do when writing an answer of more than one paragraph. Begin with an introductory paragraph that previews your answer. Follow with additional paragraphs. Begin each with a sentence that contains your main point, and follow with sentences that support your point. End your answer with a paragraph that states your conclusion.

Now use what you have learned in the **Organize/Write** step to answer the following essay test item:

Describe what you should do each day when following the five-day test preparation plan.

1. List the facts here.

2. Create a graphic organizer.

3. Now write your answer to the essay test item.

QUOTE: Time Step

6-8

T **Time** is the fourth step in the **QUOTE** strategy. For this step, you must decide how much time you should spend answering each item. Here are guidelines to follow:

- Consider how much time you have to complete the essay test.
- Consider the point value of each item.
- Write in front of each item the amount of time you plan to spend answering it. Allow more time for items that count for the most points.
- Allow some time to review your answers.
- Make sure that the time you allow for answering and reviewing does not exceed the total time you have for the test. If it does, revise your planned use of time.

Pretend you are going to take a 100-point essay test with four items. The first item is worth 40 points and the others 20 points each. You have one hour to take the test. Answer the following:

1. What is the total time for taking the test?

2. Which item counts for the most points?

3. How much time do you plan to use for each item and review?

   Item 1

   Item 2

   Item 3

   Item 4

   Review

4. Is your total planned time one hour or less?

5. What should you do if your planned time exceeds one hour?

QUOTE: Evaluate Step

E **Evaluate** is the fifth step in the **QUOTE** strategy. For this step, evaluate the content of what you wrote, its organization, and your writing mechanics.

Circle YES or NO for each of the following to evaluate your essay test answer in 6-7.

Did I answer all parts of the item?	YES	NO
Did I include all the relevant facts?	YES	NO
Are all my facts accurate?	YES	NO
Is my answer clearly organized?	YES	NO
Is my handwriting legible?	YES	NO
Did I spell words correctly?	YES	NO
Did I use correct punctuation?	YES	NO
Did I use correct grammar?	YES	NO

What could you have done to improve your answer?

Multiple-Choice Test Items 6-10

Multiple-choice test items may be written in two forms. Both forms have a stem and several answer choices. The first form gives an incomplete statement followed by answer choices. You are to identify the choice that correctly or best completes the statement. Study the following example:

stem	After President Reagan was shot in an assassination attempt, the _______________ was passed requiring a five-day waiting period for purchase of handguns.
choices	a. Adams Bill b. Brady Bill c. Kennedy Bill d. Reagan Bill

The second form has a question followed by answer choices. You are to identify the choice that correctly or best answers the question. Study the following example:

stem	The Brady Bill requiring a five-day waiting period for the purchase of handguns was passed as a result of the assassination attempt on which president?
choices	a. James Garfield b. John F. Kennedy c. Ronald Reagan d. Harry S. Truman

Use the following information to write a multiple-choice test item for each of the two forms.

The United States has a bicameral legislature. This means that the legislature consists of two houses, the Senate and the House of Representatives. Of all the states, only Nebraska has a unicameral (i.e., one-house) legislature. Each state, regardless of its population, is represented in the U.S. Senate by two senators. By contrast, the number of representatives each state sends to the House of Representatives is based on that state's population.

Incomplete Statement Followed by Answer Choices.

1.

a.

b.

c.

d.

Question Followed by Answer Choices.

2.

   a.

   b.

   c.

   d.

3. Use information from one of your textbooks to write a multiple-choice test item for each of the two forms.

Improving Your Score on Multiple-Choice Tests

6-11

Here are some guidelines you should follow to improve your score on multiple-choice tests. Read the guidelines and select an answer for each multiple-choice item that follows.

- Read the stem with each possible answer choice to decide which one to choose.
- When you read the stem, keep in mind that words like *not*, *false*, and *incorrect* can completely change its meaning.
- When you decide an answer choice is not correct, draw a line through it.
- Do not change your answer unless you are certain you made the wrong choice. Your first answer is most often correct.

Choose the best answer choice for each item.

1. ______________ an answer choice when you decide it is incorrect.
   a. Choose
   b. Reread
   c. Rewrite
   d. Cross out

2. Change an answer only when you are sure it is:
   a. too long
   b. too short
   c. the wrong choice
   d. correct

3. Which one of the following words is not likely to change the meaning of a stem?
   a. help
   b. not
   c. incorrect
   d. false

4. Which of the following should you read with each answer choice to decide which choice is correct or best?
   a. first word in the item
   b. last word in the item
   c. stem
   d. longest word

More Ways to Improve Your Score on Multiple-Choice Tests

6-12

Here are some more guidelines you should follow to improve your score on multiple-choice tests. Read the guidelines and select an answer for each multiple-choice item that follows.

- Answer all items unless there is a penalty for guessing.
- If two answer choices are opposites, one is likely to be correct.
- An answer choice is likely to be incorrect if it contains an absolute term such as *all, none, always,* or *never.*
- An answer choice is likely to be correct if it includes language used by your instructor or found in your text.

Choose the best answer choice for each item.

1. An answer choice containing the word _______________ is usually incorrect.
a. sometimes
b. usually
c. always
d. rarely

2. Do not answer items you are unsure about when:
a. you are running out of time.
b. the item is difficult.
c. the item is confusing.
d. there is a penalty for wrong answers.

3. When two answer choices are _______________ , one of them is probably correct.
a. parallel
b. opposites
c. complicated
d. long

4. An answer choice is probably correct if it contains:
a. words found in popular magazines.
b. language used by your instructor.
c. information from a newspaper.
d. words you do not understand.

Improving Your Score on True/False Tests 6-13

Here are some guidelines you should follow to improve your score on true/false tests. Read each guideline and answer the question.

1. Choose FALSE if any part of a statement is FALSE.

   Columbus discovered America in 1504.

   Why is this statement FALSE?

2. Choose TRUE only if all parts of a statement are TRUE.

   Costa Rica, France, and Nicaragua are nations located in Central America.

   Why is this statement FALSE?

3. Negative words such as *not* and *don't* can completely change the meaning of a statement.

   The United States is a democracy.
   The United States is not a democracy.

   The first statement is TRUE, and the second is FALSE. Why?

4. Items with two negatives are difficult to understand. To understand them you should cross out both negatives. Cross out the negatives in the following:

   You can not achieve a college degree if you do not pass all required courses.

   Why is it easier to answer this item when the negatives are crossed out?

5. Absolute statements are usually FALSE. Qualified statements are usually TRUE.

   All bacteria are harmful to people.
   Most bacteria are harmful to people.

   Why is the first statement FALSE and the second TRUE?

Testing What You Learned about True/False Tests

6-14

Take this test to see how well you learned the guidelines in 6-13 for improving your score on true/false tests.

Directions: Circle TRUE or FALSE for each of the following.

TRUE FALSE 1. A negative such as *not* can change the meaning of a statement.

TRUE FALSE 2. Statements with a qualifier such as *some* are usually FALSE.

TRUE FALSE 3. If a statement has two negatives, you should cross out both before answering.

TRUE FALSE 4. For a statement to be TRUE, everything in the statement must be TRUE.

TRUE FALSE 5. If you cannot prove a statement FALSE, consider it TRUE.

TRUE FALSE 6. Absolute statements are usually TRUE.

Apply what you have learned as you answer the following:

TRUE FALSE 7. All foods contain undesirable amounts of fat.

Why did you choose your answer?

TRUE FALSE 8. A balanced diet is not important for good health.

Why did you choose your answer?

TRUE FALSE 9. Alaska, Delaware, Hawaii, and New York are within the continental United States.

Why did you choose your answer?

Improving Your Score on Matching Tests **6-15**

Here are some guidelines you should follow to improve your score on matching tests. Read the guidelines and complete the matching test that follows.

- Read all the items in both columns before making any matches. One column may have more items than the other.
- Start by making the easiest matches.
- Cross out items in both columns after making a match.
- Make all correct matches before guessing at any matches.
- Make your best guess for any remaining matches.

Directions: For each term, write the letter that shows its definition.

Terms	*Definitions*
___ 1. quorum	a. group of individuals with common interests
___ 2. democracy	b. individuals who reside in an area from which a representative is elected
___ 3. aristocracy	c. individual who originally brings a lawsuit to court
___ 4. constituency	d. minimum number of members needed to conduct official business
___ 5. faction	e. system of government that gives power to the people
___ 6. plaintiff	f. system of government in which control is based on rule of the highest

Did you read all the items in both columns before making matches?

Did you start by making the easiest matches?

Which were the easiest?

Did you cross out items in both columns after making a match?

Did you have to guess at any matches?

Which ones?

Improving Your Score on Completion Tests

6-16

Each item in a completion test consists of a statement with part of the statement missing. The missing part is shown by a blank line that can be anywhere in the statement. One or more words can be missing. On the blank line, you have to write the information that completes the item.

Here are examples of completion items with the missing part in different places.

- The department within the U.S. government that is responsible for making foreign policy is the Department of ______________ .
- The Department of ______________ is responsible for the U.S. government's education programs.
- Within the U.S. government, the Department of ______________ keeps labor statistics.

Here are some guidelines you should follow to improve your score on completion tests. Read the guidelines and complete the completion test that follows.

- Read the statement and *think of what is missing*.
- Write an *answer* that *fits* the *meaning* of the statement.
- Be sure the answer *fits* the *statement grammatically*.
- If the length of the blank lines varies, *use the length as a clue* to the length of your answer.
- *Reread* the statement with your *answer* in it to make sure it makes sense.

1. If the length of the blank line varies, use the ______________ as a clue to the length of your answer.
2. Write an answer that fits the meaning of the ______________ .
3. ______________ the statement with your answer in it to make sure it makes sense.
4. Read the statement and think of what is ______________ .
5. Be sure the answer ______________ the statement grammatically.

ANSWER KEY

6-1 Paragraphs written by students will vary, but should contain the following:
1. Ask my instructor what will and will not be on the test.
2. Ask my instructor what type of items will be on the test.
3. Begin studying for the test early.

6-2 Day 5. Review and highlight important information.
Day 4. Rewrite highlighted information.
Day 3. Use remembering techniques to remember the information.
Day 2. Create anticipated questions and write answers.
Day 1. Review questions and answers before the test.

6-3 **D** Read test **Directions** carefully.
E Examine test to see how much there is to do.
T Decide how much **Time** to spend on each item.
E Answer **Easiest** items first.
R Review answers.

6-4 1. [describe], 2. [Explain], 3. [discuss]. Essay questions students write will vary.

6-5 1. relationship. 2. evaluate. 3. diagram. 4. trace. 5. contrast. 6. list. 7. summary. 8. critique. 9. compares. Essay items students write will vary.

6-6 Direction words should not vary. Focus words underlined by students may vary.
1. The <u>Constitution</u> of the United States is a set of written laws and principles. [Explain] what the <u>Founding Fathers</u> set out to <u>accomplish</u> when they wrote this document.
2. Exercise should be an important part of everyone's life. [Describe] the <u>ways</u> in which <u>exercise</u> can <u>help</u> one lead a <u>longer, healthier, and more fulfilling life</u>.
3. <u>Controversy</u> still exists regarding whether the United States was right to engage in the <u>Vietnam War</u>. Considering different views, [trace] the <u>events</u> that <u>led to this war</u>.
4. Construct a [diagram] that shows the <u>incremental effects of group size on relationships</u>.
5. A <u>cognitive view of persuasion</u> has largely replaced the <u>traditional view</u> of persuasion. [Compare] these <u>two</u> views.

6-7 1. Students should list the facts from 6-2. 2. Students should use a topic–list or series of events graphic organizer to organize these facts. 3. The written answers should contain the important information from 6-2.

6-8 1. 60 minutes or 1 hour.
2. Item 1.
3. Answers will vary.
4. Answers will vary.
5. Revise planned use of time.

6-9 Student responses will vary.

6-10 1. Students must write an acceptable multiple-choice item using an incomplete statement followed by answer choices. 2. Students must write an acceptable multiple-choice item using a question followed by answer choices. 3. Questions will vary.

6-11 1. d. 2. c. 3. a. 4. c.

6-12 1. c. 2. d. 3. b. 4. b.

6-13 1. Part of the statement (year) is incorrect.
2. All three countries are not located in Central America. France is located in Europe.
3. Because the word *not* indicates that the United States is something other than a democracy.

4. Because the statement is easier to understand.
5. The first statement is false because it contains the absolute term *all*. The second statement is true because it contains the qualified term *most*.

6-14 1. True. 2. False. 3. True. 4. True. 5. True. 6. False. 7. False. It contains the absolute term *all*. 8. False. A balanced diet is important. The negative *not* changes the meaning. 9. False. Everything in the statement is not true. Hawaii is not part of the continental United States.

6-15 1. d. 2. e. 3. f. 4. b. 5. a. 6. c.
Remaining student responses will vary.

6-16 Students do not have to answer the examples of completion items. For your information, the answers are: 1. length, 2. statement. 3. Reread. 4. missing. 5. fits.

CHAPTER SEVEN

Managing Time and Space

OBJECTIVES

1. **Teach students to evaluate and improve their study habits and study place.**
2. **Teach students a strategy for managing time.**

REPRODUCIBLE ACTIVITIES

7-1 Evaluating My Study Habits
7-2 Improving My Study Habits
7-3 Evaluating My Study Place
7-4 Improving My Study Place
7-5 Managing Time
7-6 Semester Calendar
7-7 To Do List
Answer Key

USING REPRODUCIBLE ACTIVITIES

Here is a plan for using the chapter reproducible activities. Students may complete activities either independently or in class.

1. Use 7-1 and 7-2 to have students evaluate their study habits and tell how they will improve those habits identified as needing improvement.

2. Use 7-3 and 7-4 to have students evaluate their study place and tell how they will improve those features identified as needing improvement.

3. Use 7-5 through 7-7 to show students how to manage their time by using a Semester Calendar and a daily To Do List.

Evaluating My Study Habits 7-1

Good grades don't just happen—they come as a result of good study habits. Use this rating scale to evaluate your study habits. Read each statement. For each, circle 1, 2, or 3.

STUDY HABITS RATING SCALE

Statement	*Rarely or Never*	*Sometimes*	*Often or Always*
I plan my study time.	1	2	3
I tell my friends not to call me during my study time.	1	2	3
I start working on time.	1	2	3
I review my notes before beginning an assignment.	1	2	3
I begin with the hardest assignment.	1	2	3
I finish one assignment before going on to another.	1	2	3
I take short breaks when I feel tired.	1	2	3
I avoid daydreaming.	1	2	3
I have a "study buddy" I can contact when I get stuck.	1	2	3
I write down questions I will need to ask my instructor.	1	2	3

Add the numbers you circled to get your total score. Use the following guide to interpret your total score.

Interpretation Guide

Total Score	*Interpretation*
20 or less	Study habits need to be improved.
21–27	Some improvement needed
28 or higher	Good study habits

Improving My Study Habits 7-2

List each study habit for which you circled 1 or 2 when completing the Study Habits Rating Scale on 7-1. For each habit to be improved, tell what you will do to improve it.

Study habit circled 1 or 2.

How I will improve it.

Study habit circled 1 or 2.

How I will improve it.

Study habit circled 1 or 2.

How I will improve it.

Study habit circled 1 or 2.

How I will improve it.

Study habit circled 1 or 2.

How I will improve it.

Study habit circled 1 or 2.

How I will improve it.

Study habit circled 1 or 2.

How I will improve it.

Study habit circled 1 or 2.

How I will improve it.

Study habit circled 1 or 2.

How I will improve it.

Study habit circled 1 or 2.

How I will improve it.

Evaluating My Study Place

7-3

How you plan your study place has a lot to do with how well you will study and learn. Use this rating scale to evaluate your study place. Read each statement. For each, circle 1, 2, or 3.

STUDY PLACE RATING SCALE

Statement	*Rarely or Never*	*Sometimes*	*Often or Always*
My study place is quiet.	1	2	3
There are no distractions.	1	2	3
There is good light.	1	2	3
The temperature is comfortable.	1	2	3
There is a large enough desk or table.	1	2	3
There is a comfortable chair.	1	2	3
It contains all necessary work materials.	1	2	3
It contains all necessary reference sources.	1	2	3
It contains adequate storage space.	1	2	3
It is available whenever I need it.	1	2	3

Add the numbers you circled to get your total score. Use the following guide to interpret your total score.

Interpretation Guide

Total Score	*Interpretation*
20 or less	Study place needs to be improved.
21–27	Some improvement needed
28 or higher	Appropriate study place

Improving My Study Place **7-4**

List the features that need to be improved in your study place. Include any feature for which you circled 1 or 2 when completing the Study Place Rating Scale on 7-3. For each feature to be improved, tell what you will do to improve it.

Study place feature circled 1 or 2.

How I will improve it.

Study place feature circled 1 or 2.

How I will improve it.

Study place feature circled 1 or 2.

How I will improve it.

Study place feature circled 1 or 2.

How I will improve it.

Study place feature circled 1 or 2.

How I will improve it.

Study place feature circled 1 or 2.

How I will improve it.

Study place feature circled 1 or 2.

How I will improve it.

Study place feature circled 1 or 2.

How I will improve it.

Study place feature circled 1 or 2.

How I will improve it.

Study place feature circled 1 or 2.

How I will improve it.

Managing Time 7-5

To get everything done you need to do, prepare a **Semester Calendar** for the entire semester and a **To Do List** for each day.

Semester Calendar

The **Semester Calendar** is a long-term planner and should be prepared at the beginning of each semester. Keep a Semester Calendar to record the dates on which your assignments and projects are due. Also record the dates on which you will take tests and quizzes. Carry it with you each day. Revise the calendar as the semester goes on. You can use the Semester Calendar shown on 7-6 or purchase one whose format you prefer.

Frequently review your Semester Calendar to identify the assignments and projects that will soon be due. This monitoring will help you budget your time so you complete assignments and projects on time. Monitoring also keeps you aware of test and quiz dates so you can plan your study time.

To Do List

Each night, prepare a **To Do List** like the one shown on 7-7. Write down the things you must do the next day. For example, on Sunday night you should write on the To Do List things to do on Monday. On Monday, cross out things as you do them. Add other things you must do as they occur. Include things not accomplished on Monday on the To Do List you prepare for Tuesday. Add new things that have to be done on Tuesday. Continue this process throughout the week.

You might find it helpful to use a system to code the importance of each thing to do. For example, you could put 1 next to things you *must* do and 2 next to things you *should* do but that could be done another day.

Answer these questions:

1. Why should you keep a Semester Calendar?

2. Why is it important to review your Semester Calendar?

3. What should you write on a To Do List?

4. What should you do for things on your To Do List that you did not do?

Semester Calendar

7-6

Month ____________ Year ____________

Sunday	Monday	Tuesday	Wednesday	Thursday	Friday	Saturday

To Do List

Month ____________________ Year ____________________

	To Do Monday	To Do Tuesday	To Do Wednesday	To Do Thursday	To Do Friday
AM					
PM					
Eve					

ANSWER KEY

7-1 Students' scores will vary.
7-2 Answers will vary.
7-3 Students' scores will vary.
7-4 Answers will vary.
7-5 Answers should include:

1. To record dates assignments and projects are due, and dates for tests and quizzes.
2. To complete assignments and projects on time and to plan time for studying for tests.
3. Things you must do the next day.
4. Include them on my next day's To Do List.

7-6 Students should complete and maintain a Semester Calendar.
7-7 Students should complete and use To Do Lists.

Bibliography

Barclay, D. A. (1995). *Teaching electronic information literacy: A how-to-do-it manual*. New York: Neal-Schuman.

Barton, W. A. (1995). *Outlining as a study procedure*. New York: A.M.S. Press.

Cahffee, J. (1995). *The thinker's guide to college success*. Boston: Houghton Mifflin.

Chickering, A. W., & Schlossberg, N. K. (1995). *Getting the most out of college*. Boston: Allyn and Bacon.

Conan, M., & Heavers, K. (1994). *What you need to know about developing study skills, taking notes and tests, using dictionaries and libraries*. Lincolnwood, IL: National Textbook Company.

DiYanni, R. (1997). *How to succeed in college*. Boston: Allyn and Bacon.

Ellis, D. (1994). *Becoming a master student*, 7th ed. Rapid City, SD: College Survival.

Faldenberg, P. R. (1994). *Fifteen days to study power—The do-it-yourself study skills course for high school and college students*, 3rd ed. Winston-Salem, NC: Greencrest.

Feldman, A. M. (1996). *Writing and learning in the disciplines*. New York: HarperCollins.

Ferrett, S. K. (1996). *Connections: Study skills for college and career success*. BurrRidge, IL: Irwin Mirror Press.

Flippo, R. F., & Caverly, D. C. (1991). *College reading and study strategy programs*. Newark, DE: International Reading Association.

Gardner, J. N. (1995). *Your college experience: Strategies for success*, 2nd ed. Belmont, CA: Wadsworth.

Hamachek, A. L. (1995). *Coping with college: A guide for academic success*. Boston: Allyn and Bacon.

Kells, E. C. (1993). *Taking notes in the classroom: A guide to higher grades, preparation for exams, reduced study time, less stress*. Seattle, WA: Publishers Northeast.

Knight, T. O. (1993). *Study strategies for college*. Homewood, IL: Richard D. Irwin.

Kornhauser, A. W., & Enerson, D. M. (1993). *How to study for high-school and college students*, 3rd ed. Chicago: University of Chicago Press.

Langan, J. (1994). *Reading and study skills*, 5th ed. New York: McGraw-Hill.

Leamnson, R. N. (1995). *Learning your way through college*. Belmont, CA: Wadsworth.

Longman, D. G., & Atkinson, R. H. (1994). *College learning and study skills*, 4th ed. St. Paul, MN: West.

Maker, J., & Lenier, M. (1997). *College reading with active critical thinking*, 5th ed. Belmont, CA: Wadsworth.

McWhorter, K. T. (1996). *Study and critical thinking skills in college*. New York: HarperCollins.

Mendrinos, R. (1994). *Building information literacy using high technology: A guide for schools and libraries*. Englewood, CO: Libraries Unlimited.

Pauk, W. (1993). *How to study in college*. Boston: Houghton Mifflin.

Pirozzi, R. C. (1995). *Strategies for reading and study skills*. Boston: Houghton Mifflin.

Rathus, S. A., & Fichner-Rathus, L. (1994). *Making the most out of college*. Englewood Cliffs, NJ: Prentice Hall.

Reynolds, J. (1996). *College success study strategies and skills*. Boston: Allyn and Bacon.

Shepherd, J. F. (1996). *RSVP: The college reading, study, and vocabulary program*. Boston: Houghton Mifflin.

Sotirou, P. E. (1996). *Integrating college study skills: Reasoning in reading, listening, and writing*. Belmont, CA: Wadsworth.

Starke, M. C. (1993). *Strategies for college success*. Englewood Cliffs, NJ: Prentice Hall.

Strichart, S. S., & Mangrum, C. T. (1993). *Teaching study strategies to students with learning disabilities*. Boston: Allyn and Bacon.

Van Blerkom, D. L. (1997). *College study skills: Becoming a strategic learner*, 2nd ed. Belmont, CA: Wadsworth.

Walther, D. R. (1994). *Toolkit for college success*. Belmont, CA: Wadsworth.

Whitmore, M. (1996). *Empowering students: Hands-on library instruction activities*. Lancaster, PA: Library Instruction Publications.

Wood, N. (1995). *College reading and study skills*. Fort Worth, TX: Harcourt Brace.

MANGRUM-STRICHART LEARNING RESOURCES

Order Form

Study Skills and Strategies Assessment - College Level (3S-C)
Special 50% Discount Offer!

Ordering Information:

Schools:	Enclose purchase order number, authorized signature and title.
Individuals:	Orders must be prepaid. Please enclose check or money order.
Teachers:	You may order as an individual or your school will be billed if you provide an approved purchase order number.

Quantity	Item	Regular Price	50% Discounted Price	Subtotal
_____	First 3S-C disk with 50 administrations	$ 49.95	$ 24.95	_____
_____	Each Additional 3S-C disk with 50 administrations	$ 29.95	$ 14.95	_____
_____	First 3S-C disk with unlimited administrations	$109.95	$ 54.95	_____
_____	Each Additional 3S-C disk with unlimited administrations	$ 79.95	$ 39.95	_____

Florida Residents add 6% Sales Tax.......... _____
or include Tax Exempt Number__________
Shipping and Handling ($ 4.95 for first disk; $ 1.95 each additional disk).......... _____

Check format desired: Windows____ Macintosh____ **TOTAL ORDER** [ ]
Please write for network license and pricing.

Method of Payment -- check one

- ☐ Check enclosed for ______________
- ☐ Money order enclosed for__________
- ☐ Bill us. Purchase order No.__________
  (Schools Only -- Purchase order with authorized signature and title enclosed)

Send all orders to:

MANGRUM-STRICHART LEARNING RESOURCES
Order Department
9841 SW 122 Street
Miami, FL 33176

Please make check or money order payable to:

MANGRUM-STRICHART LEARNING RESOURCES
prices subject to change

Thank you for your order!

A companion book containing reproducible activities,**Teaching Study Skills and Strategies in College**, is available from: Allyn and Bacon Order Department, P.O. Box 10695, Des Moines, IA 56336-0695 or call 1-800-278-3525.

Ship to: *(Please print)*

Name______________________
School______________________
Address______________________
City______________________
State__________Zip__________
Telephone No. (_____)______________

Bill to: *(Please print)*

Name______________________
School______________________
Address______________________
City______________________
State__________Zip__________
Purchase Order No.______________
Telephone No. (_____)______________

LICENSING AGREEMENT

You should carefully read the following terms and conditions before opening this disk package. Opening this disk package indicates your acceptance of these terms and conditions. If you do not agree with them, you should promptly return the package unopened.

Allyn and Bacon provides this Program and License its use. You assume responsibility for the selection of the Program to achieve your intended results, and for the installation, use, and results obtained from the Program. This License extends only to use of the Program in the United States or countries in which the Program is marketed by duly authorized distributors.

License Grant
You hereby accept a nonexclusive, nontransferable, permanent License to install and use the Program on a single computer at any given time. You may copy the Program solely for backup or archival purposes in support of your use of the Program on the single computer. You may not modify, translate, disassemble, decompile, or reverse engineer the Program, in whole or in part.

Term
This License is effective until terminated. Allyn and Bacon reserves the right to terminate this License automatically if any provision of the License is violated. You may terminate the License at any time. To terminate this License, you must return the Program, including documentation, along with a written warranty stating that all copies of the Program in your possession have been returned or destroyed.

Limited Warranty
The Program is provided "As Is" without warranty of any kind, either express or implied, including, but not limited to, the implied warranties or merchantability and fitness for a particular purpose. The entire risk as to the quality and performance of the Program is with you. Should the Program prove defective, you (and not Allyn and Bacon or any authorized distributor) assume the entire cost of all necessary servicing, repair, or correction. No oral or written information or advice given by Allyn and Bacon, its dealers, distributors, or agents shall create a warranty or increase the scope of its warranty.

Some states do not allow the exclusion of implied warranty, so the above exclusion may not apply to you. This warranty gives you specific legal rights and you may also have other rights that vary from state to state.

Allyn and Bacon does not warrant that the functions contained in the Program will meet your requirements or that the operation of the Program will be uninterrupted or error free.

However, Allyn and Bacon warrants the disk(s) on which the Program is furnished to be free from defects in material and workmanship under normal use for a period of ninety (90) days from the date of delivery to you as evidenced by a copy of your receipt.

The Program should not be relied on as the sole basis to solve a problem whose incorrect solution could result in injury to a person or property. If the Program is employed in such a manner, it is at the user's own risk and Allyn and Bacon explicitly disclaims all liability for such misuse.

Limitation of Remedies
Allyn and Bacon's entire liability and your exclusive remedy shall be:

1. The replacement of any disk not meeting Allyn and Bacon's "Limited Warranty" and that is returned to Allyn and Bacon or
2. If Allyn and Bacon is unable to deliver a replacement disk or cassette that is free of defects in materials or workmanship, you may terminate this Agreement by returning the Program.

In no event will Allyn and Bacon be liable to you for any damages, including any lost profits, lost savings, or other incidental or consequential damages arising out of the use or inability to use such Program even if Allyn and Bacon or an authorized distributor has been advised of the possibility of such damages or for any claim by any other party.

Some states do not allow the limitation or exclusion of liability for incidental or consequential damages, so the above limitation or exclusion may not apply to you.

General
You may not sublicense, assign, or transfer the License of the Program. Any attempt to sublicense, assign, or transfer any of the rights, duties, or obligations hereunder is void.

This Agreement will be governed by the laws of the State of Massachusetts.

Should you have any questions concerning this Agreement, or any questions concerning technical support, you may contact Allyn and Bacon by writing to:

Allyn and Bacon
Simon and Schuster Education Group
160 Gould Street
Needham Heights, MA 02194

You acknowledge that you have read this Agreement, understand it, and agree to be bound by its terms and conditions. You further agree that it is the complete and exclusive statement of the Agreement between us that supersedes any proposal or prior Agreement, oral or written, and any other communications between us relating to the subject matter of this Agreement.

Notice to Government End Users
The Program is provided with restricted rights. Use, duplication, or disclosure by the Government is subject to restrictions set forth in subdivision (b)(3)(iii) of The Rights in Technical Data and Computer Software Clause 252.227-7013.